DATE DUE

9575322 JUN 2 0 2000

REVISIONING
ENVIRONMENTAL
ETHICS

REVISIONING
ENVIRONMENTAL
ETHICS

OOO

DANIEL A. KEALEY

State University of New York Press

Published by
State University of New York Press, Albany

© 1990 State University of New York

Printed in the United States of America

For information, address State University of New York
Press, State University Plaza, Albany, N.Y., 12246

Library of Congress Cataloging-in-Publication Data

Kealey, Daniel A., 1949-
    Revisioning environmental ethics / Daniel A. Kealey.
        p.   cm.
    Includes bibliographical references.
    ISBN 0-7914-0277-0. — ISBN 0-7914-0278-9 (pbk.)
    1. Human ecology—Moral and ethical aspects. I. Title.
179'.1—dc20   89-19678
                                                                  CIP

10 9 8 7 6 5 4 3 2 1

CONTENTS

FOREWORD

No sane person would deny that we are facing an ecological crisis of global proportions—an environmental crisis that, unlike any other in the long history of our planet, has been triggered solely by our human species. The question is: What can we do about it? This implies a more subtle question that is seldom asked with sufficient rigor and honesty: *Why* do we have an ecological crisis?

The strength of Daniel Kealey's *Revisioning Environmental Ethics* lies precisely in that he cares to ask the second question and, more than that, dares to proffer an answer.

In the course of the past several decades of slowly growing ecological awareness, all kinds of solutions have been proposed to deal with the problem. For the most part these solutions have been little more than stop-gap efforts to treat the symptoms rather than address the cause. They have not been anchored deeply enough, and therefore they have by and large proven ineffective in stemming the environmental devastation occurring on a planetwide scale.

For instance, we can blame Exxon and a negligent captain for the disastrous oil spill in Alaskan waters. But surely the causes lie far deeper: They are tied in with our entire way of life that necessitates the shipping of massive quantities of crude oil over long distances. How is it possible for large corporations to exist that are environmentally irresponsible or that ignore the human dimension of their operation? How is it possible for an individual with an apparent alcohol problem to be in such a position of responsibility? How is it possible for vessels carrying such potentially hazardous cargo to be so little seaworthy? How is it possible for the government to step in only belatedly and then ineffectually?

The Alaskan tragedy is symptomatic of a whole lifestyle, a way of thinking about life, that is at the root of all the other hundreds and thousands of disasters that together amount to what we call the environmental crisis. What we find when we look closely enough is that the ecological problem is part of a much larger and far more incisive crisis. That crisis concerns the failure of a modality of consciousness that has reigned supreme in the Western countries for the past two centuries and that has exercised a largely baneful influence on the rest of the world.

This circumstance was correctly identified more than fifty years ago by the Swiss cultural philosopher Jean Gebser, whose epoch-making work is today being rediscovered by the Anglo-American world. In an intuitive flash in the winter of 1931/32, Gebser saw very clearly the bankruptcy of the contemporary Western mode of viewing the world, which he later called the "rational structure of consciousness." He also saw how the breakdown of that dominant mode did not signal the end of human civilization but harbored the seedlings of a new style of consciousness and culture—the "arational-aperspectival-integral consciousness." From Gebser's perspective the ecological crisis is thus merely the outward manifestation of a profound inner, or spiritual, malaise.

To appreciate what kind of ecological proposals could possibly make a difference at this late hour, we must look more closely at their ideological or, more precisely, their psychohistorical moorings—that is, the particular worldview or sensibility from within which they are formulated. In this book Daniel Kealey does just that. He examines different ecological models and identifies the primary structure of consciousness behind them, highlighting their potentials and limitations.

Availing himself of Gebser's model, Kealey provides an overarching framework—a meta-theory—for discussing current and possible future ecological approaches. His work has, in my view, particular merit because it connects scientific thought with the great insights of certain Eastern spiritual traditions, notably the Integral Yoga formulated by the Bengali philosopher-sage and erstwhile political revolutionary Sri Aurobindo.

Kealey boldly argues that a narrowly rational-perspectival approach to the ecological crisis suffers from severe limitations, for it operates with precisely the kind of categorical thinking that has driven us into our present cul-de-sac. He sees in the systems orientation of ecology a manifestation of the new emergent mode of consciousness heralded by Jean Gebser and, in recent years, by a host of others. By casting the spotlight on Gebser's psychohistorical model on ecology, Kealey succeeds in throwing into relief the distinctive features in the theoretical landscape of ecology. More importantly, he points to integral inceptions and possibilities that need to be developed for the necessary revisioning of the art and science of ecology, which, Kealey rightly insists, must be augmented into a full-fledged "eco-yoga."

I very much hope that this important book will raise the ecological dialogue to a new intensity so that we can heal our home planet . . . and ourselves.

GEORG FEUERSTEIN, M. LITT

Co-Director, California Center for
Jean Gebser Studies

INTRODUCTION

That the world as a whole is facing the gravest environmental crisis that civilization has ever encountered need hardly be elaborated. Daily our newspapers remind us of ever worsening problems as ozone depletion, air pollution, contamination of drinking water, the loss of vital wetlands to rampant development, the ravages of acid rain, the greenhouse effect, our overproduction of garbage, species extinction, disappearance of rain forests, the proliferation of pesticides, the dying oceans, and so forth. Then there are the many problems which the media has not decided to disseminate, such as the drastic depletion of top soil, overpopulation, increasing chemical damage to the human gene pool and immune system, the environment-destroying effects of the contemporary meat eating diet, to name but a few.

What is even more scary than these lists of plights, however, is our seeming lack of will to rectify them. The government's response is largely one of denial, of band-aid fixes and smug bureaucratic complacency and PR-disinformation that it is on top of things by enforcing (ineffective) regulations. Though there are some indications that governments are abandoning the stiff upper lip of outright denial at the time of this writing (the end of the Reagan era) we will see that denial comes in layers: "Yes, there are these grave environmental problems, but we cannot afford to budget the requisite remedy." Denial in the business world needs no comment.

Given both the gravity of the problem and our insufficient resolve to stem the tide of ecological collapse, there is, therefore, reason to feel pessimistic about the future of civilization—and, some would say, of the world itself.

The only alternative to the literal end of the (human) world would be that the end that we are approaching is not that of the world as such, but of a worldview.

Worldviewing, the way we envision the world, determines our values and, hence, also the way we live in this world, including the way we structure our economic systems. While I acknowledge the force of the Marxist argument that economics has a determining influence on ideology, I maintain that in the final analysis it is consciousness that constructs paradigmatic contexts that form the guiding principles of concrete actions. The first thesis of this book is that our present mode of world viewing does not match what is in fact reality, and that the environmental crisis is evidence of the dissonance between world and worldview. Our will is loyal to this worldview responsible for environmental degradation, hence, impotent to overcome its unintended effects.

It follows that if our world-visioning itself is myopic and unsound, any attempt to formulate an environmental ethic by way of manipulating the concepts, values and definitions of that worldview will fail to provide a realistic and adequate guide to deal with our environmental problems. What is needed is a revisioning of our relationship to nature and, consequently, a revisioning of environmental ethics. My focus in this work is an attempt to delineate the principal dynamics of visioning, the subjective source of thought and action, the premise being that the quality of environmental action and lifestyles unfold spontaneously from their visionary, or, as I will characterize it in the latter half of this book, their contemplative matrix.

In chapter 1 I delineate a psychohistorical schema of the succession of world-visionings developed by consciousness as worked out by Jean Gebser. This schema is crucial to the thesis of this book, but some readers may be put off by a theoretical orientation that makes little reference to environmental ethics per se. They could start with chapter 2 and come back to the beginning for contextual clarification of my arguments.

Chapters 2 and 3 critically examine dominant forms of environmental ethics, namely utilitarian and deontological approaches, and some alternative approaches in opposition to the former, particularly Deep Ecology and the Eco-philosophy of Henryk Skolimowski.

Chapters 4 and 5 are again a theoretical interlude that provides the background for the revisioning of environmental ethics in chapter 6. The focus in chapter 4 is precisely on *theoria* which in Greek means visioning or contemplation, as the matrix of world-visioning and world-building. Chapter 5 draws on the wisdom of Sri Aurobindo's

Integral Yoga in the attempt to find out what it would take to arrive at a comprehensive grasp of reality, of the total ecology, and to realize our most effective role in it. Chapter 6 applies these insights towards a revisioned, integral environmental ethic.

The book is a revision of my doctoral dissertation at the State University of New York at Stony Brook. It still bears some of the weaknesses of a dissertation, particularly the long and numerous endnotes. However, the rewards that the diligent reader will get by flipping back to the notes will more than counterbalance the inconvenience involved.

I wish to thank the following persons for their criticisms and suggestions: Professors Antonio de Nicolas, David Dilworth, and Peter Manchester of SUNY-Stony Brook, and Robert C. Neville of Boston University; Georg Feuerstein; and the readers and editors of SUNY Press. Completion of this book was facilitated by a Faculty Research grant from Towson State University.

○ 1

ENVIRONMENTAL ETHICS AND PSYCHOHISTORY

The environmental crisis is perhaps the final indication of the end of the modern era and the inadequacy of its guiding values for human action today and the foreseeable future. This essay is not primarily intended to add to the mountain of criticisms of the modern Western worldview and its constituent expressions, but rather attempts to identify, delineate and interpret certain philosophical expressions appearing on the edges of its cultural meta-paradigm which endeavor to give birth to a new guiding vision. These voices are not totally outside the modern meta-paradigm or they would not be as seriously considered as they are by a growing number of philosophers. Nevertheless, to speak of paradigm boundaries is philosophically significant, which this dissertation hopes to make clear in the field of environmental ethics. First, boundaries must be defined: that is what this chapter will attempt to do. Chapters 2 and 3 will then analyze representative environmental philosophers in respect to these boundary characteristics. The remainder of this work addresses itself to those characteristics which from the psychohistorical framework adopted here will most likely form the basis of an effective ecological ethic.

The ecological crisis has often been characterized as a crisis of perception: due to the myopia of perception-shaping cultural determinants people simply do not see that they are inseparable from the delicate web of life that their own actions are in disharmony with and consequently destroying. Overcoming the environmental crisis necessarily entails that they do come to see this. The question then remains how will people come to see differently. The how involves both consideration of means—which we could group under the category of education—and of ends—what shape the new perception will take. The latter leaves open the possibility that seeing their ecological embeddedness may not necessarily inspire people to act in conformity to the perceived requirements for continual optimal, or even bare survival, deferring instead to the fatalistic imperative of their current energy addictions, perhaps consoling their guilt with rationalizations and hope of Apocalytic resurrection. Indeed, the accumulated momentum of Western civilization's mission of disenchantment and demythologization has been so successful that any attempt to reimbed Western man into nature sufficiently to make him respect its harmony may prove impossible. Leaving aside the possibility of this tragic trajectory I will assume that it is not inevitable, if for no other reason than there are many indications of other possibilities already unfolding. Furthermore, I believe that revisioning our end is educational, that it will influence the means by which perception is shaped.

This belief is based upon the ecological insight that means and ends cannot be separated as we have wonted to separate them, as when we use means that "incidentally" pollute the environment in order to concretize the good life which, as a result, becomes itself polluted and thus negated. From an ecological point of view, there is no point outside of nature on which we can take a stand in order to use nature as a means towards some end. The opposing view is based on either a narrow view of nature (one that excludes human culture) or on what Kant called the transcendental fallacy, treating the supernatural as some kind of nature which we can then choose and oppose to the (lower) natural.[1]

Ecology, being one of the newest of scientific disciplines, is not as burdened with the dualistic and atomistic outlooks sedimented in the other scientific traditions. Its synthetic nature makes it interdisciplinary and holistic in outlook, and these factors constitute a worldview in which both means and ends turn out to be the same: harmony, or unity-in-diversity.[2]

Harmony, however, is a very broad concept that masks the complexity of our dynamic nature, one in which there is constant disequilibrium producing different types of consequent harmonies. In order to understand any ecosystem the ecologist must see it in terms of dynamic spatial relationships and historical patterns. The ecosystem being investigated has evolved from certain origins and is undergoing both micro and macro changes, immediate and short-term changes as well as long-term changes and long-term evolution, all the while bordering on, communicating and intersecting with, and nested in, other open ecosystems.[3]

If one acknowledges that this picture is true, then ethical implications follow.[4] The ethical interpretation of nature's ecology could perhaps be formulated: respect the integrity of nature's ecosystems as you would respect your own (i.e., those comprising your own individual integrity) for they are of warp and woof. Now that the spell of Darwinism has been lifted from our vision we are much more aware that cooperation has been more responsible for evolution than competition. In value terms, ecology stresses intrinsic value. Values emerge from some ecosystem (of which human language is a member) and are either ecologically sound or not, in which latter case they are resisted or worn down by the harmony-tending integrity of all other affected ecosystems. This is admittedly a broad, and some would contend, empty, generalization. Coupled with an integral sensitivity to the ecological balance of nature, however, it can provide a guidance for ethical decisions. The alternative to this ethical view would amount to some sort of dualism in which value is extrinsic to nature and nature's resistance to these values is not interpreted to mean that the values are unsound but that nature is evil.[5]

However, even when values are acknowledged to be natural (in the integral sense advocated here) and intrinsic, value clashes occur. In the interaction of individuals and ecosystems, extrinsic values become a factor, and on the palimpsest of the overlapping trails of time values emerging from different historical experiences compete with each other. One way of identifying worldview boundaries is by distinguishing the way time is operating in each one. It is particularly the temporal conditions that contextualize values and our perception of values which this essay attempts to clarify.

It has now become commonplace that time is not monolithic but relative. It is less well understood that there are more or less well defined modes of temporal consciousness in the world. The plurality of these modes is obscured by the predominance of the modern rational mode, with its linear, mechanical, future-directed consciousness of time, the mode which has become well entrenched over the past four centuries, and which has largely displaced the cultivation of ot!.er mode of consciousness. The other modes have not disappeared altogether, however, and continue to exert their effects surreptitiously, as in the manner of "the return of the repressed." They also become readily noticeable when observed sufficiently, a task facilitated by the fact that different temporal modes are associated with the different "faculties" of our consciousness, namely the visceral modes of instinct and emotion as well as imagination and feeling in addition to reason. Just as we associate our present era as dominated by reason and its characteristic experience of time, so can we associate previous eras with a predominance of imagination or feeling and their respective temporal modes of being. The study of these relationships is called by some psychohistory. Jean Gebser can perhaps be credited as having written most extensively about psychohistory.[6]

In *The Ever-Present Origin*, Gebser delineates the history of human civilization as a history of the unfolding of consciousness. This unfolding of consciousness is neither linear nor haphazard but can be characterized as constituted, so far, by four great "mutational leaps." Each leap marks the boundary of a consciousness structure. These structures have unfolded more or less successively from the "origin." The successions are primarily a matter of predominance, for the sublated structures continue to exist and operate in the subconscious, although no longer in the same efficient mode as when they were in turn predominant.

In chronological order, the structures of consciousness identified by Gebser are the archaic, the magical, the mythic, the mental (the present mode most closely associated with modern Western civilization), and an emerging structure which he calls the integral. Before examining the characteristics of these structures more extensively, a sense of the structures can be had with the following table:

ARCHAIC: in which the human has not yet emerged from animal consciousness.

MAGIC: the unity of all things as mediated through emotion and expressed instinctively.

MYTHIC: the awakening of soul through differentiation characterized by polar complementarity as mediated by imagination; past-oriented.

MENTAL: characterized by discursive thought and will, duality, reconciliation through synthesis, and future-directedness.

INTEGRAL: characterized by diaphaneity, suprarationality and integrality.

Gebser warns against interpreting these structures as levels of a linear progress or evolution of consciousness in which each successive level is superior to the superseded level. That would be a one-sidedly mental-rational interpretation (whereas a mythic interpretation would see them as a devolutionary series). These are appropriate judgements within their respective structures, but Gebser wants not to succumb to the dictates of the dominant mental, nor to champion a mythic or magical outlook but to transcend the limitations of these perspectives. Transcendence of the limitations of these structures complemented by a liberation into a harmonious creative expression of all the structures constitute the characteristics of the integral structure which Gebser expects to supersede the mental. When considered integrally the evolution of consciousness is seen to be omnidirectional: none of the structures is allowed to suppress the others, but each of the structures of consciousness are recognized as co-present and allowed equal participation in the unfolding of conscious experience. Gebser held that the very attempt at bringing the other (i.e., other than the mental which now has the monopoly) structures of consciousness into awareness concretizes the emerging integral structure of consciousness.

Knowledge of the characteristics of the structures of consciousness facilitates the recognition of the degree of their influence in any given cultural expression. In this investigation we are primarily concerned with how different formulations of ecological philosophy are influenced by these temporal or psychohistorical structures (they are temporal both because historical and because in assuming characteristic meanings of time they condition our experience of space-time differently, hence psychohistorical). Since, historically, we live in an era characterized as mental-rational (rational referring to the latter, deficient phase of the mental-rational structure), it is to be expected that the thought of ecological philosophers are conditioned by this structure. That is probably true for the majority of such philosophers at this time, particularly those whose orientation in moral theory is utilitarian or deontological. However, not all philosophers who express themselves in the modes of discourse developed in the mental structure completely adhere to the assumptions and perspective of this structure: one may be more closely attuned to the magical, another to the integral structure, etc.

Although most of the work being done today in environmental ethics exhibits the style and outlook of the mental structure, there has been increasing dissatisfaction with the mental basis for approaching environmental ethics, primarily on the grounds that since the environmental crisis is largely engendered by the mental structure itself, means developed within that structure to negate the damaging effects of its impact on the environment are constitutionally incapable of success; at best they can apply some brakes onto the nihilistic momentum of the technological system, but they are powerless to effect a halt to its self-destructive direction.[7] Among those who believe this to be the case, the most common reaction is to look for another structure of consciousness from which to construct a positive environmental ethic. In metaphysical thinking, for example, this turn can be seen in Heidegger who steps back to the inception of the mental-rational structure, that is, to its mental phase, when thinking was still somewhat diaphanic to mythic numinosity. The Romantic connection of some nature-loving philosophers takes them even further back than the mythic to the magical with its Garden of Eden appeal. I find this orientation among Deep Ecologists, for example. Some thinkers make the more difficult move to what they perceive as an emerging structure of consciousness (more difficult because of the climate of contemporary pessimism towards what appears to be humanistic hubris). I will examine Henryk Skolimowski in this regard.

Before proceeding with this method of categorizing environmental philosophers, acknowledgement of the limitations of this approach must be made. It suffers from the mental tendency to make clear-cut differentiations where the territory is always more ambiguous and overdetermined. Although this hermeneutical model will be used as rigorously as feasible, there is probably more art to it than science. It is commonly observed that thinkers oftentimes resist being pigeon-holed, even when the characterization seems accurate to others familiar with their position. This resistance may, in part, come from the feeling that the fixable aspects of one's thinking ride upon a more fluid and multidimensional unity which for the thinker may be the motivation, essence or intention of his mental expression and which rigid categorization alienates from one's articulated position. Gebser's psychohistorical method of categorization is not so procrustean, however, for all the structures are co-present even though one is predominant.

Another reason for resistance to categorization is that it forces one to look at one's presuppositions in a more or less objective way, and such meta-consideration often has the uncanny effect of changing one's relation to one's own position. This transformative function of categorization is one that is shared with the practice of contemplation (*theoria* in Greek) which through cultivating psychological objectivity enables or effects a transformed intimacy. It follows that this view of category employment is a process one (more precisely, an integral one) which denies the myth of the detached scientific observer in favor of the participant-observer whose observations have a transformative effect on the events being observed and vice versa: one's observing is a contemplative or self-transforming process.[8]

ORIGIN AND THE ARCHAIC STRUCTURE

The title of Gebser's book, *The Ever-Present Origin*, would lead one to expect to find much importance placed there on the origin or *arche* of consciousness. This expectation is disappointed, however, at least in terms of amount of explication. Gebser says so little about it that the naturalistically inclined reader might confuse it with the archaic structure of consciousness. Origin is not a structure of consciousness, however. It is the originary, in the sense of spiritual, presence that is both the foundation of the structures of consciousness that unfold in space-time as well as that which continuously exerts a sort of pressure on them to unfold. This pressure acts to intensify consciousness. As consciousness internalizes this pressure, tension is built up, as it were, until consciousness is forced to adjust, this adjustment being its reorganization in a new structure. Origin, is not, from the phenomenal point of view, equally ever-present at all times, however. It is most present, it seems, at those critical periods of cultural development in which a new structure or reigning worldview is born. Every mutational leap is preceded by a step back to origin which is wholeness.[9] As such it is the ever-present arche or matrix of all consciousness structures:

The concept of mutation as a discontinuous process, on the other hand, and its transposition into consciousness, underscore the originally present spiritual content in consciousness from origin. Every consciousness mutation is apparently a sudden and acute manifestation of latent possibilities present since origin.

... origin, being pre-spatial and pre-temporal, presentiates itself in the respective consciousness mutations, intensifying and integrating them.[10]

Philosophically, Gebser's view of the ever-present origin probably makes him an idealist, but whether of a dualistic type in which the origin is something like the will of God, or of a monistic type, in which it would be the One or Absolute, is not clear in the *Ever-Present Origin*. To my knowledge he refrains from acknowledging any such orientation, and I suspect would argue that such an identity is too mental whereas his approach is integral and to describe the integral in terms of the mental is to not see it at all.

The first structure of consciousness per se that Gebser identifies is the archaic, which he characterizes as one of unitive consciousness (which is not the same as perfect identity, which applies to origin). Gebser identifies it as "akin, if not identical, to the original state of biblical paradise: a time of complete nondifferentiation of man and the universe."[11] The regulative principle of consciousness in the archaic is instinct, which is to say that action is field-determined rather than originating from individual agents.

Where there is no differentiation made there is only the whole. Since humans do not differentiate or distinguish themselves from the whole there is no human soul as such. Gebser singles out a line from Chuang Tzu that is indicative of this origin-consciousness: "Dreamlessly the true men of earlier times slept." Where there are no dreams there is no soul, for dream is the medium of soul.[12] Gebser finds confirmation in the fact that early Chinese language did not differentiate earth and sky. "The soul," says Gebser quoting Aristotle, "comes into being simultaneously with the sky."[13]

THE MAGICAL STRUCTURE

The magical structure arises as an initial "fall" or departure from archaic harmony or identity with the whole. This differentiation marks the first stirring of the process of consciousness, although in its beginnings consciousness could only be characterized as completely sleep-like. Sleep-like consciousness is the initial step towards the individualization of consciousness, but being still unseparated from the whole it is unable to attain the dissociation from nature necessary to grasp it objectively. While the magical consciousness feels itself in nature, this immersion is not one of identity, but one of unity. According to Gebser, unity is identity weakened by differentiation and as such is conditioned with an element of ambiguity and insecurity. The ambiguity stems from the weak strength of sleep-like consciousness situated between the undisturbed identity of its source in the archaic structure and the individuated consciousness that the soul will approximate in the mythic and decidedly achieve in the mental structure. The configuration of this consciousness is such that neither objects nor subjects achieve independence. Aspects of the whole appear to consciousness not as separate things but as the whole; hence the characterization of the magical world as one of *pars pro toto.*

Gebser calls these partially individualized aspects of the whole "points." They are the points at which magical man faces the world, and the totality of these points, whether objects, deeds or events, constituted his system of associations. Though separate from one another they are points in the overall unity, and could be interchanged with each other. Gebser characterizes it as:

> a world in which all things and persons are interrelated, but the not-yet centered Ego is dispersed over the world of phenomena. Everything that is still slumbering in the soul is at the outset for magic man reflected mirror-like in the outside world. In a sense one may say that in this structure consciousness was not yet *in man himself*, but still *resting in the world.*[14]

The interchangeability of all things is effected by a vital nexus, not a rational, causal one. Things are in sympathy with one another; the tenor of the magic structure is one of nature realized in emotion. The emotional equivalent to the ambiguity of consciousness is ambivalence. The "participation mystique" of magical humankind is not experienced as an unqualified good in which it is desired to lose oneself. The freshly emerging impulse towards individuation is in constant threat of being overwhelmed and retaken into the womb of the forces of nature. In order to protect this nascent independence, magical humankind had to stand up to nature, appease her, attempt to exorcise her, to guide her. In these attempts to protect their limited sense of independence of nature, magical humankind began to become conscious of their will. The will developed and propped itself through magical ritual, witchcraft, sorcery, totem and taboo. These are the natural means by which humankind sought to free itself from the transcendent power of nature, through which, according to Gebser, the soul strove to materialize within humanity and to become increasingly conscious of itself.[15]

Gebser's magical structure covers, he warns, many stages, the later forms of it being quite changed from the earlier ones. The later forms of magical consciousness involve increasing reaction to nature and, therefore, further deployment away from complete unity. Magic becomes increasingly a counterspell to the spell of nature, such that the experience of unity is increasingly shifted over to the tribal ego. In the magic structure we see, therefore, the urge to freedom and, as a result, the need to be against something (the whole or nature, or whatever represents it particularly in its negative, consciousness-swallowing aspect). This "being-against" creates the separation which constitutes the possibility of consciousness. In other words, the magical structure adumbrates modern man's alienation from nature and the technological arsenal (machine magic) employed by the modern will to secure our sense of independence, freedom, and intensity of consciousness.

The temporal nature of magical consciousness is actually one of timelessness as well as one of spacelessness. Only in a spaceless and timeless world, thinks Gebser, can the point-related unity be a working reality. In the spaceless and timeless unity any point is interchangeable with any other without any consideration of time and space or of any rational causal connection.[16]

It is rather difficult to speak clearly about spaceless-timeless experience, for the introduction of diurnal consciousness (i.e., rational consciousness) into this nocturnal (for us), somnolent, trance-like state of consciousness would automatically disturb it or at the least only see it as unreal. For many, on the other hand, the lowering of consciousness into the magical experience is accomplished at the cost of consciousness, particularly of its deliberative capabilities; hence upon reemerging from this state they would be unable to give a coherent account of it. To depict or represent something is to spacialize it; to spacialize the non spatial amounts to mentalizing the magical.[17]

For the most part, the spaceless-timeless experience of the magical structure becomes known through its effects, as when the shaman returns from his trance with healing power. In this latter case, the unifying flux of the magic depths reveals its basically vegetative energy with its power for the rejuvenation of health or whole-making which the shaman or experients bring back to the more alienated social consciousness. The still existing magical structure, however overdetermined its free operation is by the individuating will of rational consciousness, also accounts for parapyschological phenomena and their elusiveness of rational control. The temporary submersion into the spaceless and timeless unity of the magical consciousness accounts for the manifestation of phenomena such as telepathy, healing and clairvoyance (and those phenomena that according to Carl Jung are characterized by synchronicity), which defy the space-time rules operative in diurnal consciousness.[18]

THE MYTHIC STRUCTURE

Just as the bare awakening of consciousness from the nondifferentiated identity of the archaic structure led to the emergence of the magic structure with its differentiated identity or unity, so did the liberating struggle against nature, which enabled the growth of individual consciousness through an increasing awareness of the external world, lead to the emergence of the mythical structure which is characterized by an awareness of the internal world of the soul. The awakening of soul, as Plato noted, is the emergence of time. Whereas the magical structure developed as an awareness of the earth, the mythic developed as an awareness of the heavens with their cyclic rotations. The cyclic rhythm of the seasons of the year, the diurnal alternation of sun and moon, day and night, the birth to death and rebirth of living beings, in fact the cyclic pattern of the movement of all things from one extreme to its polar complement and back again to its starting point, these constitute the parameters of cyclic time and the mythic consciousness. The supraterrestial heaven finds its complement in subterrestial Hades, the zenith and nadir of psychic experience. These polarities are not yet sundered into dualities as they are in the mental structure; they are the mutually dependent poles of psychic experience without either of which such experience would be as impossible as human life without either masculine or feminine gender.

The awakening of soul comes about as the formation of increasing subjectivity. It is symbolized by the mystic, with eyes and mouth closed in silence and inward-directed contemplation. The journey inward is staged in imagination structured by the polarities of time, "the moving image of eternity." The revelations of imagination constitute the making of the psyche, its precipitation into forms visible and audible. "Myth," says Gebser, "is the representing and making audible: the articulation, the announcement, the report of what has been seen and heard . . ."[19] Myth represents the soul's unfoldment, a two-dimensional map keyed with a complementary-polar structure, of the soul's inward journey and which it acts out ritually over and over again to be imprinted as memory. Psychic experience thus has the character of being undergone, of being a recycling because determined through recollection.

Psychic or mythic experience is always inherently ambivalent; each positive always contains its complementary negative and vice versa. To overlook this ambivalency in the interpretation of any mythic symbol involves a projection of the mental need for dualistic certainty which completely misses the mythic content. In fact, the circular form of thinking expressed by the mythic consciousness can be said to always have a content whereas the linear form of mental thinking breaks out of the circle into empty space. Which is to say that actual content cannot be had unambiguously and unambivalently but only with an ambivalent complementarity which constitutes its content as soul experience, or as a revelation of the self-com-plementarity of the soul. Every symbol (from the Greek *symballein*, "to roll together, join, unify") is thus constituted by a pair of possibilities which from a mental-rational point of view are antithetic (such as life and death), but which in psychic terms form a complementary whole.[20]

The saying *(legein)* of psychic reality *(mythos)*[21] must also be understood ambivalently, in the sense of word plus silence.[22] One errs by overemphasizing one over the other. For example, thinkers of the Traditionalist school (Guenon, Schuon, etc.) overemphasize the silence, the mystical, esoteric, sometimes even the magical dimension of myth at the expense of the word; whereas Modernists over-emphasize the word, the naturalistic, exoteric, and rational dimension of myth at the expense of all that is encompassed by silence. So the word or logos of mythos cannot be understood rightly on a cognitive level only, but must be contemplated, entered into (i.e., overcoming the subject-object dichotomy) and lived imaginatively. Of course, the mythic structure itself evolved, such that in its origins the silent, the dark, the timeless, the largely visceral aspects predominate over their polar aspects, the word, the sun-like, the temporal, which pre-dominate the closer its proximity to mental consciousness.

Similarly, psyche or soul is not to be understood as equivalent to ego or personal subject, but as an experiential dimension that indwells the other, the impersonal, natural and supernatural as well the specifically human.[23]

> He who is harmonized in Atman through yoga sees the self (Atman) in all beings and all beings in the Self. The yogi sees all things in the unity of the self. (*Bhagavad Gita* 6:29)

Previously dispersed in the egoless world of magical unity, the self awakens as this egoless world is transformed (or some part of it is) into a "Thou" which educes or attracts the self into being. Self indwells the other as the other indwells one's self. The polytheistic imagination of the mythic is the school of soul-making, of inter-personality.[24]

Having characterized the magical structure as a sleep-like consciousness, Gebser characterizes the mythic as one of a dream-like consciousness. The dream is a journeying through the darkness of sleep, a journey towards awakening, which in its mature form becomes a dream of awakening in which the mental image of the world is anticipated.[25]

THE MENTAL STRUCTURE

Gebser points to three important dates in the history of the mental structure: the thirteenth century B.C., 500 B.C., and 1500 A.D. It was not until 500 B.C. in Greece that the mental structure fully manifests itself as a consciousness mutation, however, and so our exposition will begin there. The events constituting this mutation of consciousness are seen clearly in the development of philosophy as it liberated itself from the confines of the polar cycle of mythos. Discursive thought is free from the operations of imagination structured by polarities, free to direct itself to object qua object, thus substituting polarity with dualism. The subject of experience under-goes a shift from all-encompassing soul to individual subjective ego. Concomitant with this mutational shift a new world takes form, the world of man, in which "man is the measure of all things" (Prota-goras). Thinking is a man (ego) directed power in contrast to the imaginational experience of the psyche which was more in the nature of undergone experience in which man had not yet predominated over the economy of the cosmos. Man measures (from the root ma:me, which is the root also for mental, meter, matter) his world, a world that is primarily material, composed of objects outside himself with which he is confronted.[26]

From measure comes abstraction, the concept or mental idea, which replaces the mythic symbol or image. Whereas the mythic image embraced such polarities as world and humanity, the concept is at once the indication of human alienation from nature as well as the attempt to synthesize these dualities in dialectical thought. Synthesis is the attempt to make a whole of discrete parts, but the wholeness it effects is merely abstract and thus far less satisfactory than the whole-making endeavors of the mythic and magical structures. Gebser finds the triangle to be the apt sign for the mental structure which is dialectical and trinitarian in character.

The mental structure also involves the discovery of space. Greek sculpture of the sixth and seventh centuries B.C. displays a new awareness of the human body, one that is three-dimensional. Gebser claims that this new awareness formed the precondition for the full awareness of space which did not blossom until two thousand years later, around 1500 A.D. in Europe, when perspective was discovered.[27]

The mental structure did not come to western Europe through the Greeks alone, for a major element of it came through the Hebrews. In the thirteenth century B.C. Moses drove a wedge of stone and law between the decadent mythical consciousness of the cultures surrounding the Jews and their emerging demythological mono-theism. The mythic polarity of nature and divinity is sundered; God is removed transcendentally and the world is disenchanted to become a profane place to be subjugated by man. The dualism of creator and creature is firmly established and subsequent attempts to blur this dualism through reversion to mythic idolatry was severely criticized by the prophets.[28]

The consequences of this dualism are allegorized in Genesis where Adam and Eve are awakened to dualistic knowledge after eating of the fruit of the Tree of the Knowledge of Good and Evil. They become ashamed of their bodies (i.e., of the more erotic, interpenetrative experience of mythic consciousness) and are cast out of the paradise of the Garden of Eden (the ecological implications are obvious). In compensation for this fall, however, man is made master of the world put at the disposal of his needs. The Yahwism of the Hebrew prophets supplied the mental structure of the West with a religiously inspired mission of demythologizing all mythic tendencies such that the harmonization of these two structures of consciousness are particularly problematic for Western culture.

The demythologizing tendency was there also in Greek Philosophy. Parmenides' philosophy of Being incisively identifies Being with permanence, truth, space, and (especially with Zeno) dialectical thought. The mythic structure of consciousness, with its character of spacelessness (which is not measurable), is assigned to non-Being. Along with the relegation of mythos to the non-Being of opinion and nontruth goes the cultivated capacities of the mythic soul: autonoetic imagination, subtle emotion or feeling, instinctual sympathy and empathy.

In terms of time, this strengthening of the conscious involves a turning away from the past, from prehistory, and a turn toward the future, a future capable of being shaped by the will, a future capable of delivering redemption. Though the mentally oriented conception of time divides and partitions the two-dimensional circle of mythic temporicity to allow the emergence of three-dimensionality or spatial perspectivization with its correlate of spatialized or quantitative and linear time, it was not always as antithetical to mythic temporicity as it has become in its rational phase. In the presocratics, Plato, the Neoplatonists and in Medieval Christianity mental rationality tried to incorporate much of the mythic outlook. These took place in what Gebser called the efficient phase of the mental structure. Its deficient, rational phase began when time, the divider, instead of being treated as such, becomes itself the divided. Divided time is spatialized time. Thus in Descartes's system time has no proper place.

Time turned against itself led to atomization and to the modern condition of alienation and nihilism. Without a positive treatment of time, argues Gebser, spatialization leads to dissolution because it destroys the very basis of space.[29] That is, our relation to the spatial world is based on mental temporal consciousness and when this latter structure is vitiated the whole order of society's spatial relations falls apart with it. This lies at the basis of the environmental crisis.

An attempt at correcting the error of excessive atomization of time is being made in the twentieth century by Continental and process philosophers as well as by speculative scientists for whom the centrality of time as the generator of space is being articulated in various ways. The new sense of time being developed today is more appropriately considered as a characteristic of the emerging integral structure of consciousness.

THE INTEGRAL STRUCTURE

The integral structure of consciousness which Gebser sees emerging in several fields (he traces its emergence in art, music, literature, psychology, mathematics, physics, biology, philosophy, the social sciences, jurisprudence, and architecture) arises largely as an awareness of the multidimensionality of time.[30] This awareness is not the equivalent of a regression to previously dominant (mythic or magical) consciousness structures, nor is it a further progression toward rationality, though due to habitual modes of thinking much of the new mutation in consciousness is misinterpreted in terms of the familiar consciousness structures.

While it is the case that the rational mode of thought is completely dominant, in spite of (or perhaps because of) this, irrationalism (or prementalism) has legions of defenders. Irrationalism need not be overt but may exercise its influence under a rationalistic guise. Examples of this would be Freud and Marcuse, whose writings evince characteristics of the magical structure, and Carl Jung whose thought exemplifies mythic characteristics. None of these cases of regression involve an abandonment of rationality but involve rather the attempt to include the irrational within an expanded mental structure. Such attempts, according to Gebser, fail, for they not only vitiate the mental, but the magic and mythic elements that they elevate to consciousness are deficient forms of these structures.

Ideal or romantic regression to an earlier structure of consciousness is an impossibility, for conscious or unconscious syntheses (which is a mental operation) of the structures pollute them with elements of each other resulting in deficient realizations. On the one hand, modern humanity cannot discard their mental realization, while on the other, the mentalization of the magic and mythic structures weakens the mental structure with truncated elements of the former. Since the first alternative is impossible, it is the second possibility that represents the real danger for world peace and harmony at this time. Gebser cites the Nazis and other mass fanatical movements as examples of this psychic conflation.

Gebser sees the solution (actually, a transcendence) of this deficient phase of the mental structure in a mutation of consciousness such that the emergent structure can integrate all the other structures of consciousness.[31] Integration, by which he means a "fully completed and realized wholeness," is effected not on the mental abstract level, but through what he calls the concretion of time which is "the re-establishment of the inviolate and pristine state of origin by incorporating the wealth of all subsequent achievement."[32] This process will render the various structures constituting the individual transparent or diaphanous, a work which can be completed only through mastering their deficient components unveiled by insight into one's own becoming.

Gebser describes how the emerging integral structure manifests itself as an irruption of time into the modern consciousness: the three-dimensional mental-rational structure which has spatialized time to merely quantitative clock time is invaded and disrupted by the fourth dimension. Gebser gives examples of how the irruption of un-mastered time threatens to destroy space and its framework:

> In Dadaism, for example, it destroyed the structure of the sentence; in Expressionism and Surrealism it disrupted the spatial structural context, exploded the pictorial content, and mutilated the form; in psychoanalysis it is a constant threat to consciousness because of the psychic inflation and disruption of the fabric of rational thought. In biology the unmastered time initiated an unchecked increase of concern with the "life force" or *elan vital*, and for a long time biology was exposed to the danger of suffocating in an extreme vitalism. Even in physics the irruption of time has brought the threat of the ultimate destruction of matter and space, as demonstrated by the atomic bomb.[33]

Gebser observes that this new awareness of time as a problem is not one limited to the culture-makers but is a problem felt by the man in the street who "has no time." To which Gebser remarks:

> How shocked he would be if he were to realize that he is also saying "I have no soul" and "I have no life!" For perspectival [mental] man, time did not yet pose a problem. Only man today who is now awakening or mutating toward the aperspectival [integral] consciousness takes note of every hour of his apparent lack of time that drives him to the brink of despair.[34]

The evolution of the structures of consciousness, from another perspectve, can be interpreted entropically, as one of a decreasing sense of security. The non perspectival and preperspectival (magical and mythic) modes provided humanity with adequate and almost adequate shelter respectively, but perspectivity provides only a fictive security, being merely a projection of security by the ego onto the external world. The fictive, merely subjective grounding of ego-boundary in itself (as in Heidegger of *Being and Time*, for whom Dasein is grounded in nothing outside of itself), brings human experience face-to-face with nothingness.[35]

The discovery/creation of the abyss of nothingness was proclaimed by the early Heidegger to be the end of metaphysics, for the goal of metaphysics has been the attainment of transcendence. Dasein achieved this transcendence by realizing that Dasein is beyond all beings, not grounded in but held out to nothing, only this transcendence led neither to God, nor to the cosmos as the sum total of all beings, nor to the ground of a Cartesian ego, but rather to nothing. In Gebserian terms, the final realization of time in terms of space, or metaphysics' realization of becoming in terms of being, brought humanity to the end of time, which is to say, to the end of mental time, and hence the end of metaphysics, the logos of the mental structure.

Whether this eventuates in the literal end of time (ecocide) or in the end of literal (quantified, antiecological) time, is the crucial question of the day. Heidegger breaks out of his earlier nihilism through which he comes to the experience of Being which he called *Ereignis*, the relational event or ultimate state of affairs which releases, lets forth and holds in their togetherness both Being and Time. Whether this can be understood as a breaking through into integral consciousness or a reversion to a quasi-mythical one is not easily decided; but it is at least an attempt to break through and as such is a *Vorsehen* or anticipation of integral realization.

The breakthrough to the integral consciousness is conceived by Gebser to come about when we are able to relinguish rational consciousness's hegemonic hold on the mental without at the same time regressing to a deficient mode.

> The courage to accept along with the mental time concept the efficacy of pre-rational, magic timelessness and irrational, mythical temporicity makes possible the leap into arational time freedom. This is not a freedom *from* previous time forms, since they are co-constituents of every one of us; it is to begin with freedom *for* all time forms. Only this form of freedom which proceeds from the concretion and integration of

all time forms, and which can be achieved only by a consciousness which is free to stand "above" the previous time forms, can bring about a conscious advance or approximation to origin.[36]

Gebser's concept of origin resembles the Neoplatonic One, the Purusha of Epic Sankhya, and the Tao of Taoism, for it is the source of subsequent consciousness structures. Instead of speaking of hypostases, Gebser speaks of mutations of time-forms from an origin itself not bound to time. It is by becoming conscious of this pregiven, preconscious, originary pretimelessness that humans attain to "time-freedom" which is not a literal return to a previous time form but an integration of present and origin in an intensified consciousness. This intensified consciousness clarifies, or renders diaphanous, all of the psychohistorical structures. The clarity of integral consciousness is not the brightness of the mental, nor the twilight of the mythic, much less the darkness of the magical, and as such does not vitiate these structures while penetrating them, but renders them diaphanous in their efficient or healthy form because harmonized or integrated with the whole. Gebser believes that one who can perceive in this manner "is free from time and can see through the whole in which he partakes, not as a part, but integrally."[37]

Using Gebser's psychohistory as a hermeneutical tool it will be possible to determine whether and to what extent a particular ecological philosophy is grounded in the magical, mythic, or mental structure. If a philosophical work cannot be assigned to any one of these structures, or a combination of them, then it is most likely to be an expression of the emerging integral consciousness. To that task we now turn.

MENTAL AND MAGICAL ENVIRONMENTAL ETHICS

UTILITARIANISM

The two most prominent approaches to environmental ethics are utilitarianism and the deontological or rights advocacy. The utilitarian approach has served as the main line of defense for environmental advocates since the beginning of the environmental movement at the turn of the century. This form of reasoning was widely promoted by Gifford Pinchot, the first American to take up forestry as a profession.[1]

Pinchot studied forestry in Germany and France, where he learned that trees could not only be protected but managed for sustained yields. The conservation movement had up to this time (1890s) largely been borne by wealthy patricians whose interest in nature were primarily aesthetic. Though of similar background, Pinchot represented the transition from the amateur tradition of nature protection to the professional and scientific management of natural resources. The utilitarian framework of his management ethic is clear in the formula which he applied to all public questions: "the greatest good of the greatest number in the long run." Unfortunately, as conservation historian Stephen Fox points out, the requirement of computability of the greatest good bore an inherent bias to measurements in board feet. This logic dealt a severe blow to the preservationist ethic, whose proponents were not disposed to measuring the worth of a pristine wilderness according to the scales of the market. Pinchot exerted great influence on Theodore Roosevelt through whom he was enabled to institutionalize the utilitarian management ethic over the entire range of federal conservation policy. In 1905 Pinchot became the first head of the United States Forest Service.

Some of the theoretical weaknesses of utilitarianism became quite apparent in the way environmental policies were put into practice. The most obvious weakness is that the defense of environmental integrity rests on its utility to man, particularly industrial man, the producer/consumer. This constitutes a procrustean grid through which all nature is forced to pass if it is to be spared from despoliation or extinction. To combat the prevailing commercial interpretation of utility, environmentalists introduced noncommercial interests, such as recreational, aesthetic and sentimental values. To their credit the consideration of these interests have gone a long way in checking commercial avarice. Despite its successes in establishing the National Park system, the utilitarian approach has steadily lost ground to the exponential increase of the high-consumption, energy-intensive, urban-industrial system. Committed to the same metaphysical assumptions and worldview of the system they are trying to protect, utilitarianists, for the most part, can only propose more of the same sorts of insufficient measures. This means increased legalistic restraints ("mutual coercion mutually agreed upon"), and increased—and more efficient—management and control of nature.

The upshot of this approach is adumbrated for us by one of its principal advocates, the ecologist Garrett Hardin. Best known to the public for his "Tragedy of the Commons," Hardin proposes increased legalistic constraint and management to protect the "commons" from environmental destruction. He compares our situation to a lifeboat, from which follows a lifeboat ethics: due to overpopulation around the world, aid to underdeveloped countries should cease and the people be allowed to starve back to their land's carrying capacity.[2]

Another important voice for the utilitarian approach was John Passmore, whose book, *Man's Responsibility for Nature*, received wide acclaim. Shortly after he published this work, however, Passmore had second thoughts about the viability of the utilitarian approach, which he thought was too anthropocentrically bound. He now called for a "new metaphysics" whose nonanthropocentric, more realistic understanding of nature would produce a more effective environmental concern.[3]

Contemporaneously with Passmore's rejection of utilitarianism, however, utilitarianism experienced a rebirth in the influencial writings of Peter Singer. His book, *Animal Liberation*, made a major impact on the moral conscience of many people when it was published in 1975, sparking a new era of activism for animal welfare. Singer's argument, taken here from his book, *Practical Ethics*, runs as follows:

Ethics comes into play when self-interest is universalized; hence utilitarianism forms the first base of any possible ethics. Universalization means that the interests of all those affected by my decision must be taken into account, where interest means anything people desire, unless it is incompatible with other desires. Universality, furthermore, assumes and necessitates the basic principle of equality, and, consequently, the principle of the equal consideration of interests. Now, the readiness to consider the interests of others should not depend on their abilities or characteristics such as intelligence, race, or sex, so long as they have the requisite characteristic of having interests. Therefore, the fact that animals are less intelligent than humans does not mean that their interests may be disregarded. Not to give the interests of animals equal consideration is to commit the moral error of speciesism, as deserving of reprobation as racism or sexism.

That animals have interests, Singer argues, is demonstrated by the fact that they can suffer, echoing Jeremy Bentham, the father of utilitarianism, who said, "The question is not, Can they reason? nor, Can they talk? but, Can they suffer?"[4] Sentience, therefore, constitutes the boundary of the principle of equal consideration of interests. Pain and suffering are bad and should be prevented or minimized irrespective of the race, sex or species of the being that suffers. Since suffering requires consciousness, however, such species and entities that are not believed to have it cannot be said to have interests that they are conscious of. Hence all species of the plant kingdom fall outside the ethical boundary. The exclusion of plant life from ethical consideration is supported by an imagination test, argues Singer:

> Suppose that we apply the test of imagining living the life of the weed I am about to pull out of my garden. I then have to imagine living a life with no conscious experiences at all. Such a life is a complete blank; I would not in the least regret the shortening of this subjectively barren form of existence. This test suggests, therefore, that the life of a being that has no conscious experiences is of no intrinsic value.[5]

Hence, not only weeds, but rivers, oceans, mountains, marshes, deserts, the atmosphere, and so forth (not to mention unconscious people), have no intrinsic value. They have no "interests" of their own. Their value is, therefore, purely extrinsic—their use-value to animals. Nevertheless, since these ecosystems are so vital to the interests of the animals that live in and depend on them, Singer's form of utilitarianism provides a fairly good ground for an environmental ethic. The weakness of his "imagination test"—it is arbitrarily based on the strength or weakness of the tester's imagination—could be corrected by positing a standard of perfect imaginative sensitivity. However such a standard transcends the arbitrariness of reason; and Singer's "imagination" is clearly a deficient one by Gebser's criterion, one that is not based on its own principles but subsumed under those of reason. This standard of perfect sensitivity will be examined in more detail in subsequent chapters on the subject of contemplation.

DEONTOLOGICAL ETHICS

Deontological ethics, or the rights view, is the major competitor of utilitarian ethics in the mental-rational structure. The major spokesman of the rights view in environmental ethics is Tom Regan. Just as Singer insists on extending equal consideration of interests beyond humans to sentient animals, so Regan insists that, as experiencing subjects of a life, animals possess inherent value, and as such have it on an equal basis with humans; therefore, animals have rights, primarily the right to live a life proper to them. This right is natural, not the result of a contract.

Regan attacks contractarianism, such as one represented by John Rawls in *A Theory of Justice*, as insufficient even for humans; it can provide no direct duties to such noncontractors as children and incompetents, thus making it not inherently wrong to hurt or kill these people. Contractors might want to prevent such violence on the basis of indirect duties to other contractors, that is, by virtue of the noncontractor's status as property or object of sentimental interest. Regan argues that this is arbitrary, making moral wrong to depend on the whim or sense of justice of contractors.[6]

Regan also criticizes utilitarianism for its inability to secure even human rights, much less animal rights. He notes that "what has value for the utilitarian is the satisfaction of an individual's interest, not the individual whose interest they are."[7] Such a reductionistic standard renders utilitarianism susceptible to sacrificing the individual for the sake of interests—property rights, for example. Thus utilitarianism as a theory can condone acts which to Regan are morally counter-intuitive. Whereas utilitarianism can justify evil means if they lead to good ends, the rights view in principle denies that we can justify good results by using evil means that violate an individual's rights.

Individual rights are based on the inherent value of an individual. To qualify as inherent such value cannot be based on relative conditions or characteristics which different individuals can have more or less of, and which consequently are to be valued accordingly. "*All* who have inherent value have it *equally*, whether they be human animals or not."[8] With the equal inherent value of animals comes their equal right to be treated with respect. Once this requirement for morality is recognized, then with the establishment of animals' rights must come the abolition of animal experiments, animal agriculture, hunting and trapping.[9]

Regan's rights view suffers from the same limitation that Singer's utilitarian approach does, namely its limitation to sentient beings. Regan claims that we do not know, and may never know, whether rocks, rivers, trees or glaciers, and so forth, are experiencing subjects of a life; hence they have no rights.

Some writers espousing the deontological approach do not, however, believe that sentience constitutes a necessary boundary of the claim for rights. They see no reason why not only humans and animals, but plant life, the soil and even so-called inanimate natural objects such as "places" should not have rights. This more universal theory of rights was first broached by Christopher Stone in an article entitled "Should Trees Have Standing?: Toward Legal Rights for Natural Objects." The expanding compass of the American concept of rights is traced by Roderick Nash.[10] In the idealism of the American

Revolution lay the seeds of the unfolding establishment of rights for all. This unfolding circle of rights extended progressively to include colonists, slaves, women, Indians, laborers, colored peoples, and in 1973, parts of nature with the Endangered Species Act.

Nash notes that Supreme Court Justice Willian O. Douglas, in a minority opinion of 1972 concerning a California ski development controversy, held that inanimate objects such as valleys, alpine meadows, rivers, lakes, even air, have a right to exist and should not be excluded from litigation to obtain that right. In support of his view, Douglas cited Aldo Leopold, a central figure in the new ecology movement, to the effect that "the land ethic simply enlarges the boundaries of the community to include soils, waters, plants, and animals, or collectively, the land."[11]

Utilitarianism and deontological ethics, the characteristic types of approaches to environmental ethics based in the rational structure of consciousness, have for the most part been anthropocentric, but have been extended by a few of their most sensitive exponents to include ever wider aspects of the whole earth. Even these latter writers have their critics who charge that their extended (rational) ethics do not go far enough, however. Some of these critics feel that the very mental-rational structure is a mistake, at least in so far as it has displaced healthier attitudes towards nature. In reaching back for these healthier attitudes in the distant past these writers base themselves in the magical structure of consciousness.

MAGICAL ECOLOGY

A discussion on contemporary magical approaches to the Western articulation of an ecological ethic must perforce operate in some kind of psychoanalytic or semiotic mode, interpreting the signs of its influence even where it is masquarading in rational disguise. Hence it is with these signs that we must begin. Because we live in and are formed by the mental structure, magical aspirations cannot be purely magical. The extent of magical influence in any given articulation is subject to interpretation. It is, therefore, with this caution in mind that I will proceed to select and interpret what I perceive as magical tendencies and potentialities. Most of these selections will be from philosophers who identify themselves as deep ecologists or ecosophists.

These nomenclatures were coined by the Norwegian philosopher Arne Naess, considered the father of deep ecology. The chief exponents of deep ecology in America are philosopher George Sessions and sociologist Bill Devall; together these three men have articulated a deep ecology platform.[12] Aspiring to be a movement, it remains to be seen whether deep ecology will broaden beyond the particular set of principles articulated by Naess, Sessions and Devall, to include sympathetic others who differ on some of these principles.

The first indication of deep ecology's nonmental (in Gebser's terms) orientation comes from its rejection of the dominant forms of environmental ethics, particularly utilitarian/natural resource management, and rights approaches. The rejection of the rights view is expressed by John Rodman as follows:

> The attempt to produce a 'new ethics' by the process of extension perpetuates the basic presuppositions of the conventional modern paradigm; however much it fiddles with the boundaries . . . [the rights movement], while holding out promise of transcending the homo-centric perspective of modern culture, subtly fulfills and legitimizes the basic project of modernity—the total conquest of nature by man.[13]

Deep ecology vents its greatest antipathy towards the utilitarian or resource management ethic, which it characterizes as shallow ecology. It is evident that this criticism is directed more to the applied utilitarianism of the management ethic than to "pure" or theoretical utilitarianism, such as the one advocated by Peter Singer. As Rodman's quote implies, however, to the extent that utilitarianism fails to criticize the basic presuppositions of the nature-degrading paradigm of modernity, so it is subject to be used by it for its own purposes. This can be seen to operate in the transformation of the concept conservation. In the radical amateur phase of conservation before the institutionalization of utilitarianism, it meant the preservation of wilderness areas, that is, to leave them untouched. Under Pinchot, however, conservation came to mean development. "There has been a fundamental misconception that conservation means nothing but the husbanding of resources for future generations. There could be no more serious mistake . . . . The first principle of conservation is the use of the natural resources now existing on this continent for the benefit of the people who live here now."[14] The commercialization of conservation is couched in such terms as "balanced use of resources," "wise use," "scientific management," "genetic improvement," and "cost-benefit analysis," forming some of the central principles of the management ideology which basically understands the whole of nature as "resources for humans."

The critique of management ideology forms one application of the deep ecology rejection of anthropocentrism. Resource conservation and development is the logical conclusion of anthropocentrism. That there has and could be more benign forms of anthropocentrism does not abrogate the fact that it is a fundamental error, that it constitutes a misperception of reality, according to deep ecology. The fundamental error consists in the belief that the human species constitutes a special case of nature, one that is above the rest of nature. This belief may justify itself through theology, philosophy, or through sheer technological will-to-power. Nature is seen as a hierarchical pecking order with man at the top. In its religious forms God is at the top, but since he gave humans stewardship over creation they are practically at the top with little but self-interest to constrain their execution of power over nature.

Philosophically, humans set themselves apart from nature by virtue of their capacity for self-reflective reason. That rationality in itself is not a sufficient much less necessary reason for establishing a moral gulf between human and nonhuman animals was argued by several ancient Greek philosophers.[15] Nevertheless, 'by reason of reason' became a foundational principle in Christian ethics when bolstered by the theological dogma that only man was made in the image of God, by virtue of which he had an immortal soul, whereas animals did not. This theological premise is as roundly rejected by deep ecology as is the philosophical one.[16]

Perhaps the most thorough arguments against anthropocentrism are made by Richard and Val Routley.[17] They argue that the various forms of the rationality criterion for membership in the "Moral Club" are found to be (1) arbitrary, and (2) insufficient even for humans. Either the criterion will not apply to all humans or it will cut across species boundaries and apply to many nonhuman animals. In the first case, it is shown that rationality is not the best criterion for membership in the Moral Club; in the second, it is shown that the restriction of membership in the Moral Club to humans only is arbitrary.

While continued refinements in rationalist ethics has remedied some of the more gross moral distortions of anthropocentrism and may hope to progress further in reform, the deep ecology critique of the type of reasoning employed in both utilitarian and Kantian ethics goes deeper to what appears to be a skepticism in regards to its viability. This skepticism concerns the inability of reason to found morality. Reason may provide some logical rationalizations for moral actions, but it can as easily provide the same for harmful actions: reason has no inherent morality. This is so especially when reason is abstracted from its total human (and nonhuman) context. Abstract reason frees itself from the economy of feeling which becomes delegitimated for ethical purposes by being denigrated as irrational. The potential of the feelings for providing the most humane and universal basis for ethical responsibility—as exemplified in the most sensitive products of moral culture, namely, saints—is limited to reduced effectiveness, if not irrelevancy, in the procrustean grid of logic. In terms of ethical development, then, deep ecology tends to see the shift to a dominant mental culture with its attendant repression of the emotional sensitivity of the magical and the feeling and imaginative sensitivity of the mythic structures as an unfortunate development, as a fall in moral sensitivity.

While the development of the mental outlook could plausibly be construed as a fall in moral sensitivity, there can be no doubt that it allowed for a progress in science. The dissociation of reason from nature allowed for the possibility of a knowledge about nature that was not to be had when the human mind was in a nondissociated state with nature. In a nondissociated state nature forms an extension of ourselves, and as such it is more or less alive and endowed with purpose. In interacting with it we cannot but get involved with its sensuous facets, and this puts limitations on our ability to exercise control over it. Dissociation enables one to interact with nature more boldly, more violently, because it is more other and, as such, requires a more invasive approach if it is to yield knowledge. Hence the rise of scientific experiment as an artificial sequestering of nature to make her comply with the project of producing knowledge. This project was facilitated by conceiving nature as a machine, which, in turn, is facilitated by thinking mechanistically, which is further facilitated by peripherizing other aspects and modes of thinking as merely subjective. The well documented progression of modern rationality from Bacon and Descartes to Auschwitz and Hiroshima has been described as the project of equating truth with utility and control. [18]

The ascent of reason, especially since the Renaissance, has been characterized by some in the deep ecology movement as the principle feature of the religion of humanism. While not unmindful of the beneficial contributions of humanism (such as its belief in the nobility and value of humankind and our achievements and competences), the deep ecologists express a deep contempt towards it. This attitude and the reasons for it are articulated by the ecologist David Ehrenfeld in his influential book, *The Arrogance of Humanism*. Though it is a secular belief, Ehrenfeld argues that the principles of humanism function like a religion in contemporary society, and it is this unacknowledged mixture of secular and religious belief that makes it the vicious influence that the deep ecologists find it to be, ". . . for some of humanism's religious assumptions are among the most destructive ideas in common currency, a main source of the peril in this most perilous of epochs . . ."[19]

The assumptions of humanism according to Ehrenfeld are:

1. All problems are soluble by people, if not by technology, then in the social world through politics, etc.
2. When things go wrong people will cooperate and solve the problem before it is too late.
3. Some resources are infinite, while all finite or limited resources have substitutes.
4. Human civilization will survive.[20]

These assumptions form part of the greater belief that the history of humanity is one of progress, especially from the time that they have liberated themselves from the shackles of superstitions that have kept them subject to nature; only then could humanity become illumined with the knowledge that they are masters of their own destiny.

Unfortunately for humanism, thinks Ehrenfeld, this heady sense of freedom where only "the sky's the limit" amounts to a delusion of hubris. Fed by spectacular short-term technological successes, humanism weaves impermeable strands of ego around the human spirit. The egoic complex is both a personal as well as a collective phenomenon. On the collective level it is constituted by the exponential growth of organization, bureaucracy, administrators and managers, whose job it is to promote efficiency which, for Ehrenfeld, amounts to finding "new ways of avoiding reality and ignoring danger, to have the power to act destructively on a large scale."[21]

"Avoiding reality" refers to the ideological reduction of coopera-tive interrelationship with nature to subjection to nature. Once the relationship has been reduced to an agonistic one, it was much easier to muster (quasi-religious, ideological) enthusiasm and willingness to sacrifice for the sake of industrialization and to "shoot for the stars" in order to reverse that perceived relationship. Egoistic hubris blinded humanism and continues to blind it to the consequences of its course of action. It fails to see, says Ehrenfeld, "that the lifestyle that makes cancer research and potential therapy remotely possible is also causing the cancer."[22]

Instead of questioning its assumptions it proposes more technology and maintains the millenniumistic promise of utopian affluence for all who would but only work for it. The tragedy of this utopian myth, claims Ehrenfeld, is that

> the overwhelming trend of the humanist-dominated present is towards more ruined soils, more deserts, more children with anomie, more sheltered, violent societies, more weapons whose horror surpasses imagination, more techniques of autocratic suppression, and more mechanisms for isolating human beings from one another. How is it possible to extract from this present reality a toil-less utopia in which technology is "the partner of man's creativity"?[23]

In other words he says, "The ultimate irony of humanism is that it has produced such a viciously inhuman world."[24]

The foregoing critical arguments of the deep ecologists clearly indicates that they are critical of the very mental structure itself, not just with this or that development within it. The fact, however, that they do engage in critical reason themsevles, puts them in somewhat of a dilemma, for critical reason is a possibility only of the mental structure. As argued in the previous chapter, however, this is unavoidable for, the mental-rational structure is the mode of discourse today within which all expression takes place however antipathic they may be in relation to this psycho-structural context. A rejection of all the forms of expression, beliefs, arguments, and so forth, of the mental structure does not necessarily place the critic outside of the structure. A philosophical skeptic, for example, probably operates almost entirely within the mental structure even while rejecting all of its assertions. But this would not be the case with deep ecology, for their positive principles clearly resonate with the characteristics of other consciousness structures. It is these we must examine next.

The ecosophists insist on a balance between reason and the so-called irrational faculties with the latter being the foundation. Since little mention is made by the chief deep ecology spokesmen of imagination, the sensitivity of the mythic structure, it would seem that the valued irrational component of their ethic consists largely of the emotional and instinctual sensitivities of the magical structure. Arne Naess, for example, talks of an "oceanic feeling" through which we are connected to the greater totality. "Without that identification," he says, "one is not easily drawn to become involved in deep ecology."[25] This feeling, furthermore, is characterized as religious, comprising fundamental intuitions of nature as living and intrinsically valuable. Intuition, of course, is one of those polyvalent words and usually means whatever is considered epistemologically fundamental. There are rational and psychic intuitions, which a deep ecologist would have no reason to deny, but these are to be founded on the truly fundamental instinctual intuition.[26] At least this is what is probably involved in the deep ecology call "to think like a mountain."

To think like a mountain could, of course, require imagination, but not the full-fledged imagination of the mythic structure; it certainly is not based on the reasoning of the mental structure. Mental intuitions not grounded in instinctual/feeling intuitions are dangerous, as evinced in the ecosophist critique of the mental structure, for they are matricidal, currently destroying the natural basis of culture at an alarming rate. Psychic intuitions are much less dangerous. They comprise the sensitivities of the agrarian soul which seeks harmony with the rhythms of nature. Even so, the agrarian revolution represents a fall from the state of innocense and non-intervening identity with nature realized by hunter-gatherers.

The hunter-gatherers typify the ecological ideal in much deep ecology literature. While an outright return to paleolithic times is not rigorously argued for, there are calls for a return in some essential respects,[27] and a return, or rather recovery, of some primitive lifestyle aspects is depicted in utopian terms, as in Ernest Callenbach's novel, *Ecotopia*. Certainly Arne Naess's desire to reduce the world's human population to one hundred million[28] could make the hunter-gathering lifestyle for all feasible again.

A second principle of deep ecology is that of biocentric equality. It holds that

> all things in the biosphere have an equal right to live and blossom and to reach their own individual forms of unfolding and self-realization within the larger Self-realization. This basic intuition is that all organisms and entities in the ecosphere, as parts of the interrelated whole, are equal in intrinsic worth.[29]

Since intrinsic worth is held to be the same in all beings, it is independent not only of its bearer's usefulness for human purposes but also of any interest, appreciation, or awareness of it by any conscious being. The refusal to acknowledge that some life forms have greater or lesser inherent value than others is to hold a position of axiological monism. Jean Gebser argues that any form of monism that emphasizes unity at the expense of real individual differences is an expression of magic feeling.

Just as magic timelessness negates real time, so does biocentrism negate the mental temporalization of evolution which tends to link the forward movement of time with progress and the development of value. This negation is seen in the writing of the naturalist John Livingston, who is often referred to approvingly by Sessions for positing a biocentric view of evolution. Livingston debunks what he calls the linear Great Chain of Being interpretation of evolution.

> Far from being an orderly determined progress, evolution is a three-dimensional searching and probing process with events occurring not sequentially but simultaneously. The direction of evolution is toward diversity, not linearity. It is quite obviously satisfying to the collective human ego, however, to see a long and orderly succession of linkages terminating with ourselves, or with a god in the anthropomorphic image.[30]

> The world of living things is not a pyramid or a tree or a ladder, with a hierarchy from "primitive" to "highest." Like all worlds the world of life is a sphere. Each point on its surface is equidistant from its center. Just as Washington and Hanoi are equidistant from the center of the Earth, the bald eagle, the Vietnam pot-bellied pig, and the human species, are all equidistant from the center of the sphere of life.[31]

So-called lower or more primitive species of plants and animals have the same inherent value as humans and as such are not merely steps toward the supposedly higher, rational life forms. The direction of evolutionary time is not upward, as it were, but implies an increase in diversity and richness.[32]

The problem of monism, axiological or otherwise, is to reconcile the one with the many. Deep ecology does not seem to see this as a problem, for the one value, life or existence, is found only in each of the many. The many is conceived under the category of species. The total quality of life is enhanced not necessarily through an increase of the many abstractly considered, but through increase of diversity of species. It is believed that the greater the diversity of species, the greater the quality of life for the beings of each of those species. We could ask the deep ecologist at this point, whether this represents an actual increase of inherent value or merely a greater distribution of the unchanged value? If there is a change, for better or worse, in inherent value, then do all the members of all the species undergo the change in inherent value simultaneously and in equal proportion, or can there be different rates of change, different experiences of time? The deep ecologist would probably not want to address this question, for to admit of deqrees of inherent value is to give license to human hubris, assuming that "give them an inch and they will take a mile."

Naess maintains that, as an intuition, biocentric equality is true in principle, but that in the process of living all species use each other for food, shelter, etc. The intuition puts a normative limit to the extent of mutual use: "We should live with minimum rather than maximum impact on other species and on the Earth in general."[33] This solution to the problem of the one and the many is not a mental synthesis or reconciliation, nor an imaginative unification by complementarity and correspondence of the mythic structure, but is a magical denial of difference.

A third principle of the deep ecology platform is that of bioregionalism. Bioregionalism stands for a movement advocating reinhabitation, cultivating a sense of place, and dwelling in a particular bioregion. These notions involve making a commitment to the land, to respect it and honor one's debt to it. The debt includes not only the recognition of the bioregion as a source of physical nutrition and the obligation to keep it healthy, but also the recognition of its role as "the body of metaphors from which our spirits draw sustenance."[34] Cultivating a sense of place through reinhabitation requires breaking the nomadic habit of contemporary commercialized culture wherein one's relationship to one's environment is reduced to circumstance,[35] and to sink roots, "sinking roots" meaning establishing a nurturing (as opposed to exploitive) lifestyle that will contribute to the health and longevity of the bioregion. The word "bioregionalism" itself is meant to convey a region governed by nature, not legislature. Kirkpatrick Sale offers the following as the essence of bioregionalism:

> To become dwellers in the land, to relearn the laws of Gaia, to come to know the earth fully and honestly, the crucial and perhaps only and all-encompassing task is to understand *place*, the immediate specific place where we live. The kinds of soils and rocks under our feet; the source of the waters we drink; the meaning of the different kinds of winds; the

common insects, birds, mammals, plants, and trees; the particular cycles of the seasons; the times to plant and harvest and forage—these are the things necessary to know. The limits of its resources; the carrying capacities of its lands and waters; the places where it must not be stressed; the places where its bounties can best be developed; the treasures it holds and the treasures it withholds—these are the things that must be understood. And the cultures of the people, of the populations native to the land and those who have grown up with it, the human social and economic arrangements shaped by and adapted to the geomorphic ones, in both urban and rural settings—these are the things that must be appreciated.[36]

Bioregionalism involves the turn towards decentralization, the liberation from distant and impersonal market forces, remote governmental bureaucracies, invisible corporation executives dictating consumer choices, while encouraging local rule and self-sufficiency. Living closer to the land fosters community, cooperation, participation. Such a lifestyle was best exemplified in the hunter-gathering societies, such as the American Indians. While the advocates of bioregionalism acknowledge that we cannot live today as did these traditonal societies, we can nevertheless learn much from them, whether it be to become future primitives or nurturing farmers.

The discussion of these three central principles of deep ecology—intuition of identity with the world soul, biocentric egalitarianism, and bioregionalism—while not exhaustive, is sufficient to demonstrate its foundation in what Gebser calls the magic structure of consciousness. This is not equivalent to saying that deep ecology is an atavistic expression or a reactionary attempt to turn back the clock, but only that it participates in the strengths and weaknesses of the magical structure.[37] These will be assessed from the point of view of the integral structure in the following chapter.

Mythic and integral environmental ethics

Mythic ecosophy

While no fully worked out mythically based ecological ethic has come to my attention, stabs at it have been made obliquely by writers concerned with the larger project of delineating the mythic nature of consciousness. One who stands out in this regard is the historian William Irwin Thompson. Thompson holds that myth is the history of the soul and as such illuminates the deep structures of consciousness in cooperative relationship with which humankind would live in harmony with nature and participate consciously in its project of evolving consciousness. The history of the ego, which is the history of civilization and masculine technology, has for a relatively limited period been able to achieve its moment of glory by repressing myth from its consciousness. The cost of egoic freedom by repressing myth, however, is that it brings Technological Man back under the sway of the collective unconscious.[1]

Thompson assumes the four ages of history developed by Vico: the Age of Gods, the Age of Heroes, the Age of Men, and the Age of Chaos. We are presently in the Age of Chaos, an age in which "our understanding of myth is quite degenerate, but the revelations of a new age of gods have already begun, and our appreciation of myth is deepening."[2] Here we see the circular view of time that characterizes the mythic structure, according to Gebser. Thompson says that the consciousness of time for the soul is synchronic, whereas for the ego it is diachronic.[3] To dance only to the diachronic beat of time is to fall out of step with the more inclusive rhythms of nature. The spirit of nature is then perceived as a monster or demon to be slain. Egoic individuation, masculine civilization and logofication (founded on writing) are the "roots of the ecological crisis of our civilization."[4]

Since the ecological crisis of civilization is the consequence of the effort to displace the female, the recovery of ecological harmony can only be achieved through a revaluation of the female, and this can only be accomplished by abiding in the whole. It is not specialized, scientific knowledge, which is about pieces, that can give us the whole; but mythology is always about the whole, the beginning and ending of things. As such, "myth is not so much an expression of one particular time as it is an expression of time."[5] Myth, Thompson appears to be saying, conserves time, whereas the phallic ego squanders it away. But this phallic independence is an illusion. Scratch the surface of scientific reason and you will see its mythic foundation. Not to treat this foundation with respectful equality constitutes a rape that is ultimately self-defeating.

Far from requiring a self decapitation on the part of science, this respectful equality would only involve a recognition of what science in effect is at a deeper level. Thompson refers to the structural anthropology of Levi-Strauss for a view of myth that takes into account all the variants of myth as a single myth without a concern for their historical context. This means "therefore, not only Sophocles, but Freud himself, should be included among the recorded versions of the Oedipus myth on a par with earlier or seemingly more 'authentic versions' . . . . All the modern schools of thought are the equivalents of variations of a myth, and all must be taken into account."[6]

While Thompson's mythological view of the origins and development of culture is very insightful, in light of Gebser's psychohistory we would question his readiness to reduce scientific thought to mythic imagination. Even the emerging integral structure would be a variant of the mythic structure. It would seem that according to Thompson, human consciousness reached its (innate?) perfection in the mythic stage of evolution, all other structures or stages of human cultural evolution being but better or worse variants of that fait accompli. In effect this would mean that the human species has ceased evolving and has become specialized, a conclusion that Thompson does not acknowledge since he holds that consciousness is evolving.[7] Since at various places Thompson does seem to broach an integral view of knowledge rather than a return to bygone mythic worldviews, Gebser's observation that the integral structure is more intimately related to the mythical just as the mental is to the magical could serve as an explanation here of Thompson's failure to adequately distinguish the emerging integral structure from the mythic and consequently undermining the very evolutionary significance of time that he wishes to posit.[8]

The difficulty in finding a mythic environmental ethic lies precisely in the mental-rational origin and character of any ethic as such. If we abandon the requirement that an ethic be philosophical (which is almost equivalent to mental-rational), then mythic approaches to ecological harmony become more evident. Perhaps the most manifestedly mythic orientation towards nature today is found in the gardening community of Findhorn in northern Scotland. There a group of people have astonished the agricultural experts by growing prize plants and vegetables under seemingly impossible conditions. Their success at growing things like forty pound heads of cabbage on basically nothing but composted sand is attributed to their cooperation with nature spirits. Some of the Findhorn gardeners claim to be able to see such mythic personages as fairies, gnomes, Pan, deities, and angelic forms of the plant kingdom. These intelligences guide the gardeners and provide unseen assistance: hence the result of so-called horticultural miracles. The Findhorn community claims that their garden should not be considered a paranormal freak but rather a vanguard marking a new age of human cooperation with the intelligences of nature, which, if taken up by humanity as a whole, would lead to heaven on earth.[9]

INTEGRAL ECO-PHILOSOPHY

Like the deep ecologists, Henryk Skolimowski[10] articulates his ecologically oriented philosophy in opposition to the dominant mode of contemporary philosophy, particularly Anglo-American analytic philosophy.[11] While there are many philosophers within the analytic tradition who are groping for new vistas, acknowledges Skolimowski, what is really needed is a new metaphysic for our time.[12] Without the prism of Gebser's hermeneutical psychohistory a disinterested reader might place Skolimowski in the deep ecology camp. Skolimowski's critique, however, does not strike one as an instinctive reaction to reason or its mental-rational structure; nor are his arguments a veiled or deliberate apology for prerational sentiments or traditional world-views. Although he does honor, and gives some play to, these factors, they do not appear to serve as the foundation for his philosophical worldview. Prima facie, therefore, Skolimowski's eco-philosophy is not traceable to either of Gebser's magical or mythic structures. That leaves either the mental or the integral as the sphere from which Skolimowski takes his presuppositions. That the choice is not altogether clear is demonstrated in the deep ecology critique of Skolimowski's eco-philosophy, the gist of which charges him with presupposing and elaborating the anthropocentrism characteristic of what we have called with Gebser the mental-rational structure of consciousness.[13]

I will argue, however, that Sessions's critique of Skolimowski is biased by his magically based worldview which fails to distinguish the integral from the mental structure; once the distinction is acknowledged then Skolimowski's integralism can be defended against the accusation that his eco-philosophy is, in effect, reducible to an ideological smokescreen for the antiecological project of the mental-rational structure.

Skolimowski sketches out what he calls an ecological humanism which, in contrast to the traditional humanism that emphasized the independence and greatness of man and his power and right to appropriate nature to his ends and needs, emphasizes instead the grounding of humanity in the scheme of nature and the cosmos. Man-in-nature, rather than the man-over-nature of Faustian humanism, reintroduces ethical imperatives into humanity's way of living in the environment which had been jettisoned with the establishment of modern industrialism, as well as some new imperatives derived from the new story of evolution.[14] These imperatives are:

1. The coming age is to be seen as the age of stewardship: we are here not to govern and exploit, but to maintain and creatively transform and to carry on the torch of evolution.

2. The world is to be conceived of as a sanctuary: we belong to certain habitats, which are the source of our culture and our spiritual sustenance. These habitats are the places in which we, like birds, temporarily reside; they are sanctuaries in which people, like rare birds, need to be taken care of. They are also sanctuaries in the religious sense: places in which we are awed by the world; but we are also the priests of the sanctuary: we must maintain its sanctity and increase its spirituality.

3. Knowledge is to be conceived of as an intermediary between us and the creative forces of evolution, not as a set of ruthless tools for atomizing nature and the cosmos but as ever more subtle devices for helping us to maintain our spiritual and physical equilibrium and enabling us to attune ourselves to further creative transformations of evolution and ourselves.[15]

The main points of contention between ecological humanism and deep ecology are summed up in the first principle. Deep ecologists wince at the call for stewardship which they charge is biased by anthropocentrism as made evident by its espousal and practice in the Judeo-Christian tradition. The argument is that stewardship inevitably leads to domination, exploitation and the ecological destruction of nature's balanced diversity. Skolimowski, however, holds that there is no denying of humanity's power and that the choices boil down to either its benevolent exercise in ecologically sound stewardship or indulgence in the short term gains of domination. Though Skolimowski acknowledges the Judeo-Christian tradition was unable to maintain the principle of stewardship, he believes that we cannot simply dismiss our long Western heritage and begin anew, but must creatively transform the tradition. He cites the process theologians, particularly Teilhard de Chardin and John Cobb, as successful transformers of the tradition.[16]

The other point which deep ecologists find noxious is Skolimowski's enthusiasm for evolution. What deep ecologists find noxious is not the fact of evolution, which they accept, but its interpretation, particularly one that places humanity at its pinnacle, as we have seen. Skolimowski does, indeed, hold that the human species is the crowning glory of evolution. To deep ecologists, however, that is merely an anthropocentric bias born of deluded hubris. The biocentric view requires instead that every species be regarded as the crowning glory of evolution. To interpret evolution in terms of hierarchy and linear progress is to see it through the procrustean frames of modernism. The deep ecology view of evolution is voiced by naturalist

John Livingston, quoted in the previous chapter.

Skolimowski concedes that up to a point his thought is anthropocentric, but only in so far as all thought is anthropocentric. All principles, he states, have been formulated and articulated by the human mind, even principles and claims made on behalf of other species or the biotic community as a whole, such as the claim of biocentric egalitarianism.[17] It is not possible, therefore, to discard all forms of anthropocentrism, though we can and must differentiate between vicious and wholesome forms of anthropocentrism and liberate ourselves from the vicious forms of it. Neither can we assume that egalitarianism is the most benevolent form of anthropocentrism nor, a fortiori, assume that the modus operandi of nature and evolution as a whole is egalitarian.[18]

The burden is then on Skolimowski to show that a benevolent form of anthropocentrism can adequately establish an (otherwise deep) ecological ethic. This is what he attempts to do with his Ecological Humanism. The central feature of nature, Skolimowski asserts, is evolution; and evolution is the origin of values. This proposition does not, as it stands, provide any clues for the derivation of an ethic, for that depends on the meaning one attaches to the term evolution. There are numerous theories of evolution, but this diversity can be simplified into groups according to the problems they attempt to answer.

Skolimowski finds that the main approaches to the phenomenon of evolution fall into five groups: scientific, epistemological, philosophical, eschatological, and cosmic.[19] Each of these approaches are of equal value and importance, hence none should enjoy priority over the others or even insist on exclusive validity. These approaches all overlap each other, Skolimowski maintains, and express the variety of aspects of our being, implying that the hegemonic assertion of one approach over the other would reduce the full measure of our being. This unfortunate possibility is, indeed, an actuality, in so far as the scientific approach to evolution has tried to appropriate the functions proper to the other approaches.

The scientific hegemony over the modern understanding of evolution has since its inception been synonymous with Darwinism. Darwin's theory was largely considered as identical with evolution itself, and still is among the public at large even though the theory is no longer held by leading biologists.[20] Assuming the materialistic belief that the universe is preeminently a physicochemical phenomenon, Darwinism conceives of evolution as a process of blind permutations, the outcome of which is designated as the survival of the fittest. To take such an understanding of evolution as the ground for an ethic would entail sanctifying the brutal and merciless in the name of survival of the fittest. Skolimowski rejects both the theory and the ethic derived from it as false.

Evolution, he states, is a frame concept or a totality concept, for it provides the boundaries and sets the preconditions for all things. A totality or frame concept defines the things it encompasses, but is not itself defined by them. The language of science is one set of the things defined by evolution, and this relation is not symmetrical. Hence evolution cannot be fully conveyed by the language of science which, after all, deals with parts and is not equipped to deal with the whole. Science finds evolution to be a phenomenon suited to scientific inquiry because it a priori assumes evolution to be so.[21] Since, however, evolution provides the great frame for all phenomena, it can as well be approached and found in the irrational as in the scientific, or in the aesthetic, the cosmological, the social, and the human. Skolimowski believes that an integrated and holistic approach to the phenomena of evolution culminates in the spiritual vision of evolution as a humanization and spiritualization of primordial matter, a vision he derives largely (more in terms of inspiration than of detail) from Teilhard de Chardin.[22]

Skolimowski, however, departs from Teilhard's Christian concept of an eternal, nonevolving perfect God, favoring instead an evolving divinity: evolution is God in the making. Though the sacred is potentially or partially in nature, it becomes actualized in human experience, not automatically, but as a result of great effort on the part of humans. it is by this effort that humans actualize their potential, which is to entertain sacredness and to participate in sacredness.[23] This sacredness which is actualized and participated in is not fixed in absolutes, but is evolution-rooted. As the highest products of the evolutionary process, the values of mankind embody the richness of past evolution but are also open-ended, pregnant with higher forms. As the cornerstones of morality, therefore, these values are neither bound to absolute forms, nor are they merely arbitrary and subjective constructions, for they are mediated through humanity, not invented out of nothing. Skolimowski sums up these values in what he calls the New Moral Imperative.[24]

- behave in such a way as to preserve and enhance the unfolding of evolution and all its riches;

- behave in such a way as to preserve and enhance life, which is a necessary condition for carrying on evolution;
- behave in such a way as to preserve and enhance the ecosystem, which is a necessary condition for further enhancement of life and consciousness;
- behave in such a way as to preserve and enhance the capacities which are the highest developed form of the evolved universe: consciousness, creativeness, compassion;
- behave in such a way as to preserve and enhance human life which is the vessel in which the most precious achievements of evolution are bestowed.

In his critique of Skolimowski's *Eco-Philosophy*, Sessions pointed to the last derivation as evidence of its anthropocentric stance. In his rejoinder, Skolimowski objected that to lift that moral precept from all the other precepts and the central thesis from which they are derived (which Sessions failed to mention), is to distort the spirit of the ethic in order to make it fit the bogeyman of anthropocentrism. He further argues that what the deep ecologist finds distasteful,[25] namely, the designation of man as the most evolved form of life, is the conclusion of almost all approaches to the phenomenon of evolution. It is not an arbitrary bias: the anthropocentric invective should not be recklessly applied. Its proper application is to positions which clearly separate man from nature and place man (him over her) over nature, especially when it is a relation of domination over. To employ the concept for a holistic, man-in-nature philosophy enjoining an ethic of deep respect for all life stretches the concept of anthropocentrism beyond sense, prompting one to suspect an emotional rather than rational use of the word, as, indeed, we wish to point out here.

While one can obtain an anthropocentric reading of the New Moral Imperative by abstracting out the last precept, one could equally obtain a biocentric reading of it by abstracting the first precept enjoining respect for evolution and all its riches. Since Skolimowski abstracts neither, however, the New Moral Imperative harmonizes the two perspectives in a holistic view which resembles mythic polarity. It is well to recall here that Gebser found a resonance between the mythic and integral structures. Structural resonance implies that it is easier for a mentally structured intelligence to relate to a magical expression than to a mythic one. Gebser noted that for the cultivation of an integral consciousness, much will have to be learned from the mythic worldview. The mental antipathy toward the mythic worldview, especially in the Judeo-Christian West, presents difficulties in the way of learning from the mythic voice, and might explain why this author was unable to find any apparently mythically based ecological ethic.

Another possibly mythic element in Skolimowski's eco-philosophy is his stress on imagination and its important role in developing an integral knowledge of the world. A close examination of his use of imagination, however, shows no indication that it might be based on, much less bound by, the mythic structure of consciousness. His overriding stress on evolution precludes the possibility that it is mythically based. While the concept of evolution is not totally foreign to the mythic worldview, it was contained within an overall circular framework.[26]

Skolimowski's most sustained treatment of evolution centers around epistemological concerns. He outlines a new epistemology corresponding to the new picture of reality being developed by quantum theory or the New Physics, against a background of Karl Popper's (under whom he studied at Oxford) conjectural philosophy. Popper, whose philosophy signalled the demise of the structurally rigid logical empiricism, argued that all knowledge was conjectural and tentative and is founded on a process of relentless criticism rather than on an infallible foundation built of atomic facts and propositions. While acknowledging that Popper's pluralistic epistemology and open-ended rationality was very refreshing and fruitful, Skolimowski finds that it (including the extension of Popperian philosophy in Feyerabend and Lakatos) is less and less helpful for the newly emerging epistemological problems of quantum physics. The reason for this is that Popper's central notion of empirical refutability presupposes that there is a firm and unequivocal nature 'out there' against which conjectures can be found to be contradictory. The picture of reality emerging from the New Physics, however, contradicts the assumption that there is a given reality out there which is prior to and independent of the mind that grasps and describes it. The correspondence theory of truth is undermined when the separation of mind and reality is denied, when reality is conceived as coextensive with the mind, when the picture of reality is one of an indeterministic, open, participatory universe.[27]

One of the New Physicists Skolimowski draws from is Jean Charon who gives mathematical demonstrations of the existence of what we have called "mind" in atomic particles. In his theory called Complex Relativity, Charon posits matter, or the visible, as Forms which constitute the Real, and the meaning of Form, or the invisible, as Symbols which constitute the Imaginary. He finds that "Forms/ Symbols are complementary aspects of the same 'uniduality', in the same way as are the corpuscular and wave aspects of any particle of matter in physics."[28] Charon states that

> the most important result of Complex Relativity is the demonstration that each individual particle of matter should be represented as possessing both of these complementary aspects of Real and Imaginary; each individual particle is made up of Forms, *and also* of significant Symbols. This means, in turn, that each individual particle has "senses" to detect the Forms of its "outer world." . . .[29]

The Symbolic is the source of free will or creativity, which is present even in atomic particles in a positive way, not negatively as in the way some use Heisenberg's Principle of Uncertainty to allow the possibility of there being free will in particles, whereas the principle merely reflects on the impossibility of the human observer's obtaining a complete knowledge of the initial position and motion of any particle.

In Skolimowski's cosmology, Charon's Imaginary is conceived as "sensitivities", a term that is to include what is normally meant by mind, imagination, and will. Sensitivities are the agency of evolution. Sensitivities, it may be said, are the monad's windows (thus making good the chief deficiency of Leibniz's monads). The more windows an entity has the greater its sensitivity to reality. Evolution is constituted by the qualitative increase in sensitivities. Sensitivities, however, are not merely passive receptors transmitting information already pre-existing 'out there'. They are also the agencies through which entities articulate, affect and mold reality. The evolution of sensitivities from the eukaryotides (which created our atmosphere) to man entails articulating the world in new ways. As new aspects are elicited from the world, sensitivities exercise the power of co-creation of reality. While receiving the aspects of reality mind always processes them, and this processing of reality aspects is at the same time a transformation of them. So-called outer reality and sensitivity are together the "uniduality" of the interactive mind. Neither the outer reality nor the mind is prior or more fundamental than the other, but both are always given together, and their togetherness is an interactive one, in which mind comprehends reality and in the act of comprehension transforms reality through its creative act.[30]

In man evolution has created so far the most complex and "glorious" power of creative sensitivities. The capacity of rational thought is a highly evolved sensitivity. Skolimowski emphasises the continuity between thinking and the entire spectrum of sensitivities that have been evolved. Thinking occurs within this context of experience, and this heritage of multifarious experience is within thought.[31] To abstract thought out of its evolutionary matrix is to impoverish it and our sensitivity to reality. Knowledge, for Skolimowski, is more than a matter of being cognitively informed, for as a function of sensitive immersion in reality, the more all of our heritage of sensitivities is brought into play, the more integral and reality-creative our knowledge is. This heritage includes such sensitivities as moral empathy and the various forms of intuition, including mystic perception. Hence, in addition to the sense of reality obtained in scientific culture, through the imaginative power of our sensitivities, we have also available to us the sense of reality obtained through the esoteric (i.e., mythic) traditions, the sense of reality obtained through so-called primitive (i.e., magical) cultures, and even the senses of reality obtained through the various animal species (the archaic and beyond).

Where Skolimowski differs from the traditionalists, including those deep ecologists who elevate the sense of reality obtained through hunter-gatherer culture, is in the belief that evolution has not ceased its struggle to create new windows on reality, or new sensitivities. New sensitivities in the making will create deeper, more rich senses of reality. We will know more of reality. Since knowledge is both transformed by and transforming of reality, Skolimowski believes evolutionary reality could be characterized as matter being transformed through sensitivities into spirit.[32]

Skolimowski asserts that evolution is a process in which reality becomes increasingly complex. Increasing complexity poses a problem for knowledge. Even though increasing complexity in the interactive universe/mind is not a one-sided affair, mental complexity does not increase at the same rate as the outer world. Mind thinks the world in paradigmatic ways and, at certain critical levels, the increasing complexity of the ontological order becomes unmanageable. In order to cope with this difficulty the mind restructures its form of thinking. Skolimowski characterizes this restructuring maneuver as *simplification*. Simplification is a key element in his "epistemology of becoming." It is the modus operandi of the human mind. Complexity/simplicity is the epistemological equivalent of reality/mind. "Complexity on the ontological level and simplicity on the level of understanding . . . are inseparable companions. We always simplify, in order to understand. Understanding *is* simplifying."[33]

Skolimowski traces out the large outlines of simplification in the history of Western thought. In the sixth century B.C. the mythological conception of reality in Greece give way to a rational conception of reality; mind imposed on reality a distinctive pattern of simplicity, which in this case is identified as *logos*. The Greco-Roman cycle initiated and controlled by logos comes to an end a thousand years later. From its disintegrating complexity emerged a new logos or understanding identified as *theos*, which shaped the psycho-social structure of the medieval cycle. The medieval theos cycle came to an end about another thousand years later in the Renaissance. The Renaissance failed to produce its distinctive logos, however. Only in the seventeenth century did a new logos emerge. Skolimowski identifies this new logos as *mechanos*. The mechanos understanding created a vigorous modern culture, but after only three centuries it is apparently no longer able to contain its contradictions within it. Skolimowski sees a new logos emerging, and he calls it *evolutionary telos*. This new pattern of simplicity, though still tenuous, is already organizing human experience and knowledge, the pattern being based on the cosmological unity of mind and reality that is inspiring a new ecological integration of humanity and its universe.[34]

The new cosmology of the participatory universe[35] will reverse our moral alienation from nature and humanity, which is to say that the sundered natural and moral orders will be reharmonized. The dualistic world view of mechanos has undermined and confused the human sense of responsibility. Responsibility entails an altruistic sense of taking care for the rest, for all of becoming in the new evolutionary cosmology. Though a logical or even natural necessity to assume responsibility cannot be so absolutely established that no one would dissent against it, Skolimowski acknowledges, the new cosmology can demonstrate its desirability even for the agent. Responsibility functions in the Platonic and Augustinian sense as the measure of human being: the more sense of responsibility that a human can cultivate, the more human he or she is, whereas to be unable to be responsible or to voluntarily give up one's responsibility is, "in a sense," to lose one's status as human being. We are enhanced by the exercise of responsibility, and we are diminished when we lack it. We have the choice: on the one hand, we can either continue to believe in the mechanistic worldview supported by a dualistic, objectivist form of thinking which, despite its intentions, undermines the values by which human life is secured and enhanced, not to mention the rest of life (variations of this choice include counsels of despair, stoicism or nihilism); on the other hand, we could embrace the new participatory universe cosmology and become its midwives through cultivating its "reverential mode of thinking" which is both based on and creative of the sense of responsibility for all things and for the future continuation of evolution. The latter choice would entail concrete changes in the socio-economic sphere in the direction of decentralization and 'appropriate technology' which would bring responsibility back to human beings.[36]

SKOLIMOWSKI AND INTEGRALISM

My treatment of Skolimowski so far shows that he is motivated neither by a mental-rational nor by a premental (mythic or magical) oriented worldview. Some aspects of his evolutionary point of view further indicated that he is likely attempting to articulate an integral view. It was argued that Skolimowski appeared to George Sessions to be defending a "revisionist" philosophy of the mental structure primarily because the latter's magical oriented deep ecology world-view fails to distinguish the mental from the emerging integral structure. Nevertheless there is some truth in Sessions' charge of anthropocentrism against Skolimowski's philosophy. This partial truth was invalidly demonstrated in Sessions' arguments, but may be elicited if, with the heuristic aid of Gebser's psychohistory, it could be shown that some of Skolimowski's assertions do entail mental presuppositions. These mental presuppositions are especially evident in his concepts of time, evolution, and God (which converge into a single concept), and I will attempt to show that they are not compatible with the integral aspects of his philosophy.

Though laced throughout with spiritual values, Skolimowski's concepts of time and evolution are basically naturalistic, for they are not framed by eternity or by the supernatural. Time, particularly evolutionary time, is the ultimate frame, as we have seen. In fact, Skolimowski goes so far as to equate evolution with God. Hence his is a pantheistic naturalism. In this respect, his position is very similar to that of Samual Alexander who presented a picture of a growing universe in which matter, life, consciousness, and so forth, gradually emerge from the space-time system (time being the mind of space) evolving towards its perfection, which he calls deity. Since the emergence of man the whole world is engaged in the production of deity. This God, like all other beings, is a creature of time. Emergent levels arise as a result of the complexification of the (lower) previously achieved level. When the physical level achieves critical complexity, life emerges, and so on, each emergent, by definition, being something new.[37]

Acknowledging that each level is an emergent, involving a qualitative *saltus* beyond the previous level, is not the same as an explanation, however. Perhaps it is the scientistic bias of naturalistic philosophies which make them back away from the metaphysical task of explanation. Their tendency to try to make description serve as explanation shows the need for the latter, however. That the world can be described as a mechanism or as an organism, or that it is the product of a holistic force which is nothing but the process of the whole organizing itself into an increasingly holistic hierarchy (Jan Smuts[38]); or that reality is a system of processes which constitute an interdependent continuum of systems which evolve into increasingly adapted and increasingly complex and individuated, hierarchically related modules (Ervin Laszlo[39]), does not tell us why this is so, nor, ultimately, how it is at all possible. Most embarrassing for these naturalistic philosophies of evolution is the positing of an evolutionary nisus or holistic force which by the constraints of their logic must be itself an evolutionary product of reality; and yet it is used to explain reality, which thus begs the question.

Skolimowski begs the same question. On the one hand he talks of nature evolving into God, while on the other hand he says evolution is God. His concept of God is one of God-in-the-making. This resembles Whitehead's consequent nature of God, only Skolimowski does not have a counterpart to Whitehead's primordial nature of God. Since man is posited to be the highest achievement of evolution to date, in effect there is no God yet in Skolimowski's worldview, though he believes there will be one sometime in the future. This hope is expressed in the concept of the Omega point, which he derives from Teilhard de Chardin but stript of its association with the Christian God. The Omega point represents evolution's point of consummation and self-perfection, when matter will have become spirit. Skolimowski also calls this evolutionary perfection Brahman Enlightenment, although at no point in his philosophy do we ever find a defined concept comparable to the Indian concept of Brahman; in which case we have Brahman enlightenment without

Brahman! Similarly, the concept of Omega point, as envisioned by Teilhard, is a unity of heaven and earth, or of the convergence of the *Pleroma*, the cosmic Christ, with the *Parousia*, the highest point of human complexity-consciousness. Being only one-half of this equation, Skolimowski's Omega point is a crippled one. It is one which reduces evolution to a miracle, in fact to a series of innumerable miracles all miraculously synchronized to produce the biggest miracle of all—the creation of God and eternity.

The conjunction or unity of time and eternity is not in itself a metaphysical impossibility, but if anything is, the emergence of eternity from time, or of God from the evolution of nature, qualifies as a candidate. One cannot pull a rabbit from a hat unless the rabbit was there in the first place, or at least the elements necessary to create a rabbit need to be in the hat in order for the miracle to occur. Skolimowski does mention evolution's potentialities, but these are given no ontological foundation. Without such a foundation, his belief that the Omega point is a potentiality for spiritual perfection cannot be distinguished from, say, the belief that from the given of our birth we have the potentiality for physical immortality. There is no basis for the production of the supernatural from the natural unless the supernatural is already the central element—in however potential a form—of the natural. A God produced in time and continually transcending itself is a universal embryo, an unfulfilled Being which cannot embrace a real end unless it realizes eternity. An eternity produced from time can only be an infinitely prolonged time, but unending time is not the same as eternity which transcends it.

So, though Skolimowski presents an eschatology of spiritualization, he provides no foundation for it. A hope for greater humanization and ecological adaptation is the highest ideal that the boundaries of his metaphysics would support. To go beyond that is to hope for a miracle.

It is quite possible, however, that Skolimowski is consciously weaving a philosophical myth designed to sustain hope. "Hope and wholeness are metaphysical foundations of our life."[40] Theology is an articulation of human hope. Human beings, in making themselves transbiological beings, produced images and symbols in which their dreams and aspirations could be vested. "These images and symbols were deified and institutionalized in various religions, and their presence helped man in his further spiritual journey."[41] It follows that deification is merely a pragmatic device or benevolent self-deception to spur mankind in the direction of their hopes, even if the end is an unattainable myth.

Such a use of myth, however, is characteristic of the mental-rational structure. We see it in Plato and Western monotheism. From the perspective of the mythic structure such a use of myth is deficient, introducing incompatible mental perspectivity into the imaginative experience of the soul. Neither is it paradigmatically mental, for it is dependent on irrational religious faith. Gebser would probably characterize this aspect of Skolimowski's thought as a deficient development of the mental structure. The mythic structure of polarity and circularity is ruptured by mental temporality which is linear, spatialized, and future-oriented. Skolimowski attempts to transcend the perspectival blinders of the mental structure but fails to realize an integral worldview; hence his eco-philosophy might be characterized as one that is transitional in regard to an integral worldview.

The integral structure of consciousness, according to Gebser, is one that is present-oriented, but a present that is diaphanic in regards to not only the future-oriented temporality of the mental-rational structure, the past-oriented temporicity of myth, and the timelessness of magic, but also of the "origin" or "a-mensional" aspect of time which is known more traditionally as eternity, the transcendent, or the Absolute.

An outline of an integral eco-philosophy will be delineated in the ensuing chapters. That elucidation will try to show that Skolimowski's aim can better be fulfilled within a full-blown integral structure rather than in one that attempts to disguise it in a quasi-mental or naturalistic one.

The integral transcendental differs from traditional Western usage, for its primary reality is not theological or rational, but a structure of awareness. It is an awareness and sensitivity to poly-dimensional reality, including the dimensions repressed under the regime of the mental-rational structure of consciousness. Hence the integral present is not the same as the present in the mental structure, nor of any other structure of consciousness. Unlike the mental, it is not just a new point on the arrow of time. Unlike the mythic, it is not merely an eternal return; and unlike the magic, it is not a timeless unity. In the integral structure these are recovered as aspects of the polydimensional present. In recovering these dimensions, which are both 'timed' and 'timing' (i.e., have both objective significance in the world that is thus revealed and subjective significance in terms of physical, passionate, moral and intellectual sensitivities), the integral structure of consciousness not only revitalizes previously developed capacities for ecological adaptation but creates new ones necessary to achieve harmony in the changed world of today.

One of the chief characteristics of the emerging integral consciousness observed or speculated by various writers, is its contemplative nature, by which is meant its transcendence of the egoistic perspective, its participation in the "other," awareness of unity-in-diversity, transtemporal awareness, transparency in regards the whole, of exhibiting a quality or impression of total presence. To portray the present of the integral structure as contemplation brings out some of its dynamism, for in the mental structure the present is almost an empty set, being merely a divider of the past and future. But contemplation also suffers from its association with the mythic structure, as a result of which its reintroduction to a contemporary ethic may seem atavistic to some. As a function of consciousness, however, contemplation is inherent in all structures of consciousness, although each structure develops a characteristic mode of contemplation. All modes of contemplation can be efficient or deficient, productive of harmony or disharmony, creative or regressive. As an expression of human consciousness contemplation is not a finished accomplishment refined in the past, but is in continuous development. Contemplative skills developed in the past will aid us in bringing to birth a contemplative realization for our time, but integral contemplation will nevertheless be a new development of consciousness, not just a repetition of old habits.

My aim in the following chapters is to outline an integral philosophical ecology that spans the ends of time as well as of space. To fulfill this I will draw from Plotinus's philosophy of nature and contemplation, and from Aurobindo's philosophy of evolution and yoga. Together these philosophers incorporate the past and future of time and West and East of space.

○ 4

PLOTINUS ON NATURE
AND CONTEMPLATION
AND THE ONE

Plotinus (205-270 A.D.) is not a name one will find often, if at all, in the literature of environmental philosophy, a neglect that it shares with contemporary philosophy generally. Besides his historical importance as a systematizer of Ancient Greek philosophy and for providing the philosophical foundation of subsequent Christian mysticism, Plotinus deserves our attention in this project of birthing an integral ecological philosophy for at least two reasons. First, his conception of consciousness is one that is much broader than the usual views espoused both in Greek and in contemporary philosophy. It acknowledges deeper levels of consciousness than the phenomenal level of awareness, levels that transcend the subject/object dichotomy that seems so absolute to so-called normal consciousness. Plotinus's descriptions of these other levels of consciousness are vivid with a sense of immediacy born of his direct experience of them. The principal levels of consciousness are called hypostases in Plotinus's system and they can be compared to Gebser's structures of consciousness: the psyche to the mythic structure, the intellect to the magical, and the One to Gebser's origin. Though Plotinus treats these hypostases from the perspective of the efficient mental structure, he has much to contribute for an integral understanding. His philosophy of contemplation is especially important for the development of an integral ecological ethic.

The second reason for his relevance to this project is that his thought is a bridge between East and West. Plotinus is known to have had an interest in Indian philosophy. Though scholars debate whether this interest had any influence on his thought it remains true that his philosophy is compatible with Vedanta philosophy. This means that Indian philosophy need not be considered foreign to Western thought, with the implication of their incompatibility. One of the benefits of studying Eastern traditions is the rediscovery of the Eastern dimension of our Western tradition that it may occasion.[1] The thinker who can thus transcend the artificial (in the sense of historically artifacted) abyss between East and West is facilitated in the attempt to break free of confinement to the (deficient, rational stage of the) mental structure and be open to an integral understanding.

Despite these relevancies of Plotinus for our project of construing an ecological philosophy, the fact cannot be ignored that Neoplatonism has been blamed for Christiandom's alienation from nature. Feminist theologian Rosemary Radford Ruether charges that Christianity's estrangement from nature was inherited from a combination of apocalyptic Judaism and classical Neoplatonism. Neoplatonism, she argues, elevates the transcendent logos of immutable Being to the status of true reality at the expense of the sensual world. This prompted Christianity to form a worldview in which nature is either dominated or rejected by spirit. As a result there developed in Christianity the alienation of the mind from the body, the alienation of the subjective self from the objective world, and the subjective retreat of the individual, who was alienated from the social community.[2] Insofar as the blame is leveled at subsequent Neoplatonists, but not at Plotinus, I will not dispute this charge. In Plotinus himself, two tendencies can be identified: one, is the transcendental, emphasizing the ascent, or "flight of the alone to the Alone"; second, is the integrative, emphasizing the immanent divine depth of this world. Perhaps in light of subsequent Neoplatonism it is the first, the other-worldly tendency, which has been overemphasized in Neoplatonic scholarship. This essay is an attempt at the alternate reading, an integral understanding of Plotinus's philosophy of contemplation. I believe that it is this alternate, immanent side of Neoplatonism, for example, that has influenced such contemporary philosophers as Martin Heidegger and Gabriel Marcel, whose thinking have been celebrated as ecologically sensitive.

Contemplation bridges the subject/object dichotomy, linking each level of reality with its corresponding level of consciousness (except in the case of the One which transcends all differentiation). Plotinus not only links the subjective and objective poles of reality in this way but states further that these subjective sides of reality are ontologically prior to their objective manifestations, these latter being likened to poor images of their archetype. Plotinus called the states of consciousness *theoria*, contemplation, and their objective manifestations *theorema*, which can be translated as either work of contemplation, object of contemplation, or result of contemplation. The world as theorema is the product of contemplation. But the world stands to contemplation not only as product, for it too contemplates. To one degree or another all things contemplate and aspire to contemplation. This is the thesis by which Plotinus begins his treatise "On Nature and Contemplation and the One."

> Suppose we said, playing at first before we set out to be serious, that all things aspire to contemplation, and direct their gaze to this end—not only rational but irrational living things, and the power in plants and the earth which brings them forth—and all that attain to it as far as possible for them in their natural state, but different things contemplate and attain their end in different ways, some truly, and some only having an imitation and image of their true end—could anyone endure the oddity of this line of thought?[3]

Interestingly, Plotinus proposes this thesis as a play. Lest we then dismiss the thesis as some rhetorical ploy, not to be taken seriously, Plotinus is quick to show that he takes this proposition very seriously. In an explanatory footnote to this text Armstrong observes that "playing" here probably refers to Plato's use of the concept in *Laws* IV 712B 1-2 (in which the interlocutors imagine the laws of an ideal city, "like elderly men playing a boys' game), and VII 803C-D (where man "has been constructed as a toy of God," and that our highest and most serious activity is to make our play as perfect as possible). Play is here proposed to be a more effective means than is seriousness for leading the inquirer into the experience of contemplation, and this probably for at least two reasons: (1) it encourages the use of imagination, and (2) it frees the mind from more or less exclusive concentration on the given conditioned sensuous aspect of objects so that the playful nature of the world in its wholeness can be fully participated in. In any case, an argument over whether seriousness or playfulness is the best approach to realize the truth should not distract one from the point that "one plays and the other is serious for the sake of contemplation." All actions of whatever type are "serious efforts towards contemplation." Obviously some types of actions will be more successful in this regard than others, and Plotinus makes the observation that those actions which are most opposite to play, namely those serious actions which we are involuntarily forced to perform are ones which most hamper the state of contemplation.

While actions are something the mind can readily grasp and understand in a positivistic or behavioral sense, this behavioristic understanding is insufficient for purposes of understanding contemplation. Contemplation is not to be reduced to the behavioristic or outwardly manifest aspect of actions without emptying contemplation of its meaning. If actions are only "serious efforts towards contemplation," then they do not fully exhibit or participate in contemplation. Actions are rather a "shadow of contemplation and reasoning."(III.8.4) People engage in action and have their minds distracted by the purely superficial aspects of manifest action because "their souls are weak and they are not able to grasp the vision sufficiently, and therefore are not filled with it, but still longing to see it, they are carried into action, so as to see what they cannot see with their intellect."(III.8.4)

To hold that actions are a shadow or image of contemplation is to bring into play a symbolic mode of knowing. A symbolic mode of knowing would try to understand actions as images of a higher life concealed in their working as their essence and origin. The main methods by which a symbolic mode of knowing is brought into play are art, by which the contemplative virtue of beauty is evoked; religious iconography, by which such contemplative virtues as piety and love are evoked; and mathematics, whose crystalline operations attune the mind to the Forms. Plotinus gives merely lip service to the Pythagorean-Platonic discipline of mathematics, but spoke highly of the power of art to lift the soul with the wings of beauty. Beauty is the domination of matter by Form, or Form made visible to the sensitive soul. Even the weak soul sunk in the dissipated consciousness of sensual action can be stirred by the power of beauty of bodies, images, music and excellent actions. Beauty is something which the soul becomes aware of even at the first glance and recognizes and speaks of it as if it understood it already.(I.6.2) It welcomes beauty and adapts itself to beauty as if it recognized beauty to be of the same nature as itself. How are beauty and soul akin, queries Plotinus?

Beauty and soul are related in so far as they are both productions of Form. It is the participation of the things of this world in Form, which have their station in *Nous* (Intellect, sometimes, under influence of the German *Geist*, translated as Spirit), that endow the things with beauty. The more completely a thing participates in Form, the more the beauty inherent in Form is manifested in its recipient nature. Conversely, the less a thing is dominated by Form, the more ugly its appearance. In the Platonic tradition Form is reality or Being. Truth, Beauty, and Goodness are the chief characteristics or Forms of Being and, consequently, the more a thing participates in, or partakes of, the experience of Being, the more it will exhibit these characteristics. "Beautifulness is reality."(I.6.6) Both Soul and the things it contemplates as beautiful or ugly have their common origin in the One, the source of Being. Intellect (Nous) is the One's first emanation or hypostasis in Being. Plotinus sometimes refers to Nous as God, that which is most like the One under the condition of the Many. The One is beyond Being, or beyond God. Hence, the true beauty of the Soul is to be found in its own highest being which is the Intellect; and to the extent that it is perfectly conformed to Intellect, says Plotinus, so is it truly soul. "For this reason it is right to say that the soul's becoming something good and beautiful is its being made like to God, because from Him come beauty and all else which falls to the lot of real beings."(I.6.6)

To posit that manifestations of beauty (the objective) and souls (the subjective) are alike by virtue of a common third element, Form, only gives us a static, logical explanation which is insufficient for portraying the more dynamic aspect of their relationship. In the treatise "On Beauty" Plotinus portrays the dynamic (*dunamis* in Plotinus is the contemplative power of the Forms) relation as one of a procession of Beauty from the One (which is also characterized as the Good) to Intellect, where it is recognizable as Beauty, and which, in turn, gives beauty to Soul, the second hypostasis. Everything else below the purely psychic (Soul) dimension is beautiful by the shaping of Soul. In fact, Soul tries to make everything it grasps and masters beautiful.(I.6.6) The psychic dimension refers not only to individual human souls but to World Soul or Cosmic Soul and to pure disembodied (abstract) soulness alike, although the latter is sometimes identified with Nous by Plotinus. In any case, beautifulness is soulness, and the beauty of this world is a reflection of Soul or the imprint of Soul, which by the power of Forms that inhere in it, gathers the dissipated and relatively unformed matter (theoremata deformed by lapse of time) into organized wholes which, relative to their less formed parts, are beautiful. Thus, whether the beautiful thing is a work fashioned by a human soul or a natural beauty fashioned by the World Soul, the beauty is in each case the work of Soul and an image of soulness. When a human soul experiences beauty it is, consciously or unconsciously, actually being stimulated by universal soulness; it is suddenly edified by its own nature which is beautiful. We might ask here, why is it that if Soul is beautiful it needs to be reminded of its inherent beauty by an extraneous sort of beauty?

The chief characteristic that differentiates Soul or Psyche from Nous is duration or time. Nous is nondurational or eternal (notwithstanding Plotinus's various contrary assertions, which he tries to justify as necessarily paradoxical, the logic of the Divine transcending the logic of science), and as such is omniscient and omnipresent, having all contents of knowledge altogether at once, which constitutes perfect contemplation. Soul, however, is unable to maintain that intellectual quietude necessary to reflect the whole at once, for it has a "restless power" which does not want, or cannot have, the whole to be present to it altogether, but prefers to experience the whole successively in one form after another in an infinite number of different ways. By thus dividing up, measuring the illimitable it loses its integrity and dissipates the unity of the whole into ever weaker extensions and part formations. Soul thus temporalizes first itself and then reality; time is the life of the Soul.(III.7.11)

The Soul's activity of "betiming" is also a work of art, for the reality which has been worked or betimed is an image of what is before time, the eternal Forms of Intellect. Time for Plotinus, as it was for Plato in the *Timaeus*, is the moving image of eternity. Time is the One contemplating under the limitations of Soul. Soul's contemplation is temporal. The essential character of the Soul's activity is contemplation of the whole under particular temporalized Forms. However, while its essence (in any particular instance) is the whole under a particular temporalized Form, the Soul's contemplation is inherently distracted and cluttered by its own past acts of contemplation, i.e. by memory and habit.

The cluttered state of mind is a problem for Soul because the intuitions of different times are not completely comformable to each other, each being the contemplation of the whole from a different perspective. An act of contemplation in the present cannot be isolated from past acts of contemplation which help constitute the present one and which thus render it as ambiguous or overdetermined. This problem obtains only under the condition of time, because for the Soul which is conformed to Intellect there would be no past acts of contemplation, Intellect being beyond severed time. At the level of Intellect, therefore, the Platonic concept of recollection would not make any sense. On that account Plotinus replaces recollection with direct intuition. Noetic intellection is beyond time and so memory is not in order there, for all is present. "Intellect, therefore, really thinks the real beings, not as if they were somewhere else; for they are neither before it nor after it."(V.9.5) There is no ambiguity in noetic intellection.

The embodied soul, however, must rely on memory in the attempt to compensate for its weakened intuition. Memory is a Soul power *(dunamis)* which weakens in direct proportion to the soul's degree of absorption in the sense level of experience. The soul's power is fully actual in Intellect, but when embodied its actuality loses ground to potentiality, which is a more passive state of being. The more the soul is merely passively perceiving and remembering the superficial appearances of things, the further it strays from seeing things in their real being. Soul only knows things completely and fully in Intellect, which is to say, when it perceives their eternal being as identical with its own being. Such knowing also constitutes the soul's actualization of its power and this, notes Plotinus, confirms Parmenides' alleged statement that "thinking and being are the same thing."[4]

Thus the soul self-limited to perceiving instrumentally through the senses is blind to real beauty, and can see only its faint reflection, matter. In order to perceive real beauty the soul must develop a "passionate love for the invisible."(I.6.4) This passion of love, *eros*, seems to be a necessary predisposition that renders the soul receptive to the ubiquitous but otherwise hidden splendor. Plotinus adopts Plato's philosophy of eros, with some minor differences. Eros in Platonism is not just a passion of deficiency seeking for satisfaction but is also a logos, which is to say that it is not merely a passive potentiality but is partly an active dunamis by virtue of its constitution as an expression of a rational principle; a delegate, as it were, from the Intellect in the world of embodied souls. Plotinus expounds his view in "On Love" as an exegesis of the myth of the birth of Eros according to Diotima in the *Symposium* (203b). In Diotima's story, Eros is depicted as the offspring of Poverty (or Need) and Plenty (or Resource). Plotinus interprets Plenty to stand for Intellect while Poverty is Soul's embodied existence. This accounts for the double nature of love, personified as the higher or heavenly Aphrodite Ouranos, who is pure, and the lower, earthly Aphrodite who is wanton. The lower behavior of love is a privative condition of love whose contemplation of what is truly most lovable has been distracted and enthralled by the superficial beauty of bodily forms.

Love is capable of privation because it is not a pure rational principle but is of mixed constitution, having

> in himself an indefinite, irrational, unbounded impulse; for he will never be satisfied, as long as he has in him the nature of the indefinite. He depends on soul in such a way that he comes from it as his origin, but is a mixture of a rational principle which did not stay in itself but was mingled with indefiniteness.(III.5.7)

Soul enthralled by bodily existence always desires but never attains, while Soul identified with Intellect "always desires and always attains; and the One neither desires, for it has nothing to desire, nor attains."(III.8.11) This is not to say, however, that the One or Good is not characterizable by love. For Plotinus the Good is not only lovable, *erasmion*, but is eros. "He is at once lovable and love and love of himself."(VI.8.15) Hence for the Soul eros is not merely the conveyance towards the Good, upon the attainment of which eros is dropped, but is the end and perfection which the soul will conform to eternally.(VI.7.22)

While Soul is naturally attracted to beauty, it is beauty in conjunction with goodness which enflames love. Beauty without goodness may either mislead the soul towards, and entrap it in, the non-being of externality (I.6.8; V.5.12), or it may leave the soul cold and unenthusiastic with a mere passionless attraction. (VI.7.22) This applies equally to intelligible as to physical beauty. The attraction exercised by the Good is primal and ubiquitously constant (because it has all power), whereas the attraction exercised by beauty is of a derivative power, not as deep, and is intermittant and relative. The power of the Good to attract need not be perceived to be effective, and it is always at work, whereas the power of beauty can only be effective when perceived.(V.5.12) Beauty, then, functions most appropriately when it is a means of experiencing an even deeper level of being, namely, the Good,

> just as with bodies here below our desire is not for the underlying material things but for the beauty imaged upon them. For each is what it is by itself; but it becomes desirable when the Good colors it, giving a kind of grace to them and passionate love to the desirers. Then the soul, receiving into itself an outflow from thence, is moved and dances wildly and is all stung with longing and becomes love . . . and is truly winged.(VI.7.22)

True eros is the love of the Good, a love which carries within it its own principle of purification and perfection. It is a logos, and as such is deeply connected with the reality underlying all things. The more life a beautiful object possesses, the more beautiful it is because life has "soul, and this because it has more the form of the Good; and this means that it is somehow colored by the light of the Good, and being so colored wakes and rises up and lifts up that which belongs to it."(VI.7.22)

The beauty of physical objects, then, is a reflection of the beauty of the Forms. But in the Intellectual or Spiritual world of the Forms themselves, Plotinus argues in VI.7.32, beauty is not just one Form as a part amongst others, but must be that which generates Form; and that which generates Form is the principle of Form and as such must be formless. Consequently,

> when you cannot grasp the form or shape of what is longed for, it would be most longed for and most lovable, and love for it would be immeasurable. For love is not limited here, because neither is the beloved, but the love of this would be unbounded; so his beauty is of another kind and beauty above beauty. For if it is nothing, what beauty can it be? But if it is lovable, it would be the generator of beauty. Therefore the productive power of all is the flower of beauty, a beauty which makes beauty.(VI.7.32)

For the attainment of this source of all desiderata, the value of all values, one "should give up the attainment of kingship and rule over all earth and sea and sky, if only by leaving and overlooking them he can turn to That and see."(I.6.7) Clearly, however, merely the giving up of social amenities and power will not bring one the Summum Bonum. "How, then, shall we find the way?" asks Plotinus in introducing the method of contemplation. "Let him who can, follow and come within and leave outside the sight of his eyes and not turn back to the bodily splendors which he saw before. When he sees the beauty in bodies he must not run after them; we must know that they are images, traces, shadows, and hurry away to that which they image."(I.6.8) Some beautiful things are better than others in effecting this purpose. Plotinus recommends that one begin by looking at beautiful ways of life and then at the beautiful moral works of virtuous persons and finally at the souls of those people who produce beautiful works.(I.6.9) The external looking at beauty must be complemented by internally-directed looking.[5]

This seeing inwardly, the seeing of beauty within one's own soul, is not a mere passive looking, but an active intervention, an education or drawing out of potential beauty, a process Plotinus likens to "working on your statue" till one sees the "divine glory of virtue" shining within oneself. Working on oneself could be understood as developing one's power, or actualizing one's potential. In the matter of the affections this would involve transforming them from their merely passive states (i.e., purely reactive to external situations) into active states, of which love is the primary exemplar.(III.5.7) An active affection is one which most exhibits the higher Soul qualities, and these qualities are Soul expressions and reflections of the perfect contemplation of Nous. Affections are more real and active the more they arise from the unitive level of Soul, which is to say, the more they approximate the contemplative power of Nous.

Plotinus's views on beauty and love illustrate the sort of symbolic knowledge that he is encouraging philosophers to bring into play when, for example, he exhorts one see physical objects as shadows of a greater reality. Because it involves faculties usually excluded from "serious" knowledge, (i.e., the passions, imagination, moral, and aesthetic sensibility), Plotinus's theory of knowledge goes beyond the prevalently cognitive views philosophers tend to have of knowledge. That is so in that he does not ground knowledge in sense perception, as do empiricists, nor in the laws of reason, as do rationalists, but finds the source of knowledge in the transcendent One whose act of knowledge is identical with himself. True knowledge is undifferentiated absolute identity. This super-knowledge, if it can still be called knowledge, is the perfection of knowledge. The nisus of knowledge on all levels of being is towards identity which is complete knowledge. The standard by which the degree of truth of any knowledge is measured is the identity of the knower and the known: knowledge is truer as knower and known become more identical.[6]

The primary model of knowledge so-called, however, is Nous, because in Nous there is plurality and differentiation, conditions usually presupposed for the possibility of knowledge. The differentiation in Nous is not opposed to unity, but expresses unity in the most perfect degree possible for any multiplicity. The simplest difference that can be generated from the absolute unity of the One is that between contemplation of the contemplator and the contemplated, theoria and theorema. In its origin this difference is a mere difference-in-unity, for in Nous the contemplator or contemplation "must be the same as the contemplated, and Intellect the same as the intelligible; for, if not the same, there will not be truth; for the one who is trying to possess realities will possess an impression different from the realities, and this is not truth. For truth ought not to be the truth of something else, but to be what it says."(V.3.5)

By identity of theoria and theorema Plotinus means not the overpowering of the latter by the former, as in epistemological idealism, but that the theoremata contemplated are themselves also theoriai or contemplations of the whole. If theoremata do not become identical with theoriai then they remain merely objects in another subject and, even if living objects, they would not be self-living. In Nous all is self-living, for Nous is the fullest life.(III.8.8) Plotinus employs images to depict this highest level of contemplation in order to provide the soul with some contemplative aids, though these images can only give an external representation which must be "dematerialized" to allow the identification of the soul and what it is contemplating to be realized. For example, Plotinus likens Nous to "something all faces, shining with living faces."(VI.7.15) Each face or Form is a particular power, which makes Nous a multiplicity, yet each is all and in perfect harmony with the whole because identical with it (which makes Nous also a perfect unity) even while remaining a part. Nous is perfect unity-in-diversity. Each maintains the appearance of a part, "but a penetrating look sees the whole in it."(V.8.4) This heaven world of Nous is not another place, but as the last quote makes clear, this very world of appearances seen with complete penetration. So heaven is this world of men, animals, plants, sea and earth, but now seen in and as Nous, heavenly.

All things There are transparent and there is nothing dark or opaque, everything is clear, altogether and to its inmost part, to everything, for

> light is transparent to light. Each There has everything in itself and sees all things in every other, for all are everywhere and each and everyone is all, and the glory is unbounded; for each of them is great, because even the small is great. The sun There is all the stars, and each star is the sun and all the others. One particular kind of being stands out in each, but in each all are manifest. (V.8.4)

Since heaven or Nous is this world as experienced in perfect contemplation, there is no type of appearance "here", however lowly or loathsome, that cannot be saved. This is to say, every existent can be experienced as having inherent divine value, but the degree to which the inherent value of things can be known depends on the degree of one's contemplative intuition. To see all things as heavenly, as the living substance of God, is not to collapse the value distinctions of all things into a single value. Distinctions in value remain on the surface of each being, in their appearance, even though in their common depth they are seen in and as oneness. Differences in value are "according to their nearness to the first principles." Hence a god is greater in value than is a man or animal because more totally Nous. Even an irrational and inanimate thing is a living thought in Intellect, and since at a deep level theoremata are identical with theoria, is "a particular kind of Nous," and as such does not cease to be Nous, and as Nous the Nous of all, although in a particular way.

> For it is actually one thing, but has the power to be all: but we apprehend in each what it actually is: and what it actually is, is the last and lowest, so that the last and lowest of this particular Nous is horse (for example), and being horse is where it stopped in its continual outgoing to a lesser life, but another stops lower down.(VI.7.9)

An important consequence of perfect contemplation, where the contemplated is the same as the contemplation or where thought and being are the same, is that whatever is thought "There" necessarily comes into being. Simply by being what it is, contemplation, Nous produces. Nous does not intend or choose to create; yet if the intelligibles subsist, the sensibles will ensue from a necessity inherent in contemplating intelligibles.(VI.7.8) Contemplation, theoria, is at the same time production, *poiesis*. In this respect Nous imitates the infinite, supremely active dunamis of the One whose formlessness is productive of all Forms and hence of the existence of all things. Plotinus emphasizes that this outflow of Reality from the One is not the work of a Creator, nor a matter of chance, but is rather a spontaneous but perfectly natural expression of the nature of the Origin, and is without temporal beginning or end. As a natural expression of the One the procession of Reality cannot terminate until everything that could possible come into existence on all the levels of being has actually done so. Each of these levels, furthermore, must be complete in its turn: Nous containing the totality of being in a timeless eternity, Psyche or Soul under the conditions of temporal succession, and sensible Nature under the conditions of spatial extension.

Poiesis, the productive aspect of contemplation, is in another view *tolma*, the impulse of self-assertion. The self that is asserting its desire for existence is always a part of its originary context. Later Neoplatonists explicated this concept to mean that spiritual beings are not created by another but come forth voluntarily from their source and shape themselves.[7] The shaping of themselves, however, comes about not from this act of self-assertion, which is a descent in the outgoing direction of non-being, but from the turn back inwards towards their source. This is the essential and primary movement of contemplation, but on all levels lower than the One, the act of contemplating one's own source is initiated from an unfavorable vantage point (on account of the tolmaic procession) and thus is productive of an inferior vision or theorema, an imitation of its source. Plotinus tends to see this tolmaic aspect of contemplation as regrettable, but not to the extreme extent of the Gnostics for whom the concept was equivalent to the principle of evil. In any case, he barely mentions this "moment" of contemplative production (i.e., the self-assertion) in his model of poiesis, according to which the best action is accomplished by the nonaction of resting in oneself. "But that true All is blessed in such a way that in not making it accomplishes great works and in remaining in itself makes no small things."(III.2.1) In moral works this principle is followed by and exemplified in the highest type of man who always does the right thing immediately and spontaneously without having to think about it. That is because his soul is intimate or united with Nous, and in Nous action and contemplation are identical, and thus in perfect equilibrium. The reason why Plotinus emphasizes the "return" moment of contempla-tion (which is self-negating, the via negativa) over the tolmaic moment of self-assertion is that with the descent of soul the former wanes while the latter waxes in strength, and philosophy must endeavor to bring these powers back into balance. Moreover, since the outward movement of self-expression happens more or less spontaneously, the key to right action is the controlling, forming element of contemplative vision, the depth of inwardness determining the rightness of outward action.[8]

As contemplation weakens, the gap between theoria and theorema, contemplation and action, becomes more marked, to the point where contemplation becomes absorbed by outer action, where action, the contemplated, becomes for all practical purposes the only form of contemplation. That is why Plotinus calls action at this level a mere shadow of contemplation. Even though it is a straying from contemplation, however, action never leaves contemplation entirely behind, and tries to return to contemplative intimacy by producing works which will be enjoyed by contemplation. Works are performed ostensibly for the preservation and enhancement of self-existence through a process of possession, and possession is a tendency towards identity or union, which is perfect contemplation. Contemplation is the end of action. The more action is attuned to contemplation the less the need of the soul to go out of itself in action (i.e., the greater the quality of action, the less the quantity of action).(III.8.6) Contemplation is both the origin and end of action, for poiesis is the application of rational Forms to potential matter, and this is an activity of contemplation, "for creating is bringing a Form into being, and this is filling all things with contemplation."(III.8.7) Hence, the originative principle (Form, Logos, contemplation) is for all things the goal, which is to say that the whole life of the universe is philosophy.[9]

That the whole life of the universe is philosophy, is known only through contemplation. Noncontemplative, dianoiaic thinking cannot understand this truth. A proper usage of dianoiaic thinking, though, such as the propaedeutic employment of comparisons, negation, and the study of things as produced from the contemplation of Nous, will enable the philosopher to make intellectual progress towards it. (VI.7.36) Philosophy proper in the Platonic tradition begins with dialectical thinking, which, writes Plotinus, is not just a philosopher's tool or a matter of employing theories and rules, as in dianoiaic thinking. Dialectic "deals with things and has real being as a kind of material for its activity," for it is the reasoning employed by Nous whose thinking is a direct intuition of the being of what it thinks. (I.3.5) As the most valuable philosophical activity, dialectic is not arrived at by dianoiaic thinking alone, but, in the words of Plotinus, we can only "advance towards It by purifications and virtues and adornings of the soul and by gaining a foothold in the world of Nous . . . ."(VI.7.36) The ascent to the true life, or rather the making manifest of the true life here in this world, is one which must be lived through, in the sense of involving the whole person in right relation to one's environment, and not just thought through.

THE RELEVANCE OF PLOTINUS FOR ECO-ETHICS

From the foregoing we can summerize at least ten points particularly relevant to an integral ecological ethic.

1. All nature contemplates. This may be the most important tenet, for it at once negates the ontological separateness of the natural, human and divine spheres. All share in and are constituted by the fundamental act of contemplation. That by which the human realizes his or her humanity and personhood is also that by which nature natures. Because of their inseparability, human well-being cannot be bought at the expense of the rest of nature's well-being. The more that human contemplation identifies with both the natural and divine dimensions of contemplation, the more will humanity both fulfill itself and allow for greater ecological harmony.

2. Action is a shadow of contemplation, that is, is a form of contemplation. Or, more technically, contemplation is the form, *eidos* or *idea*, of action, its end or telos. As such, contemplation is not something apart from, much less opposed to, action, but is that which fundamentally fulfills the aim of action, and which in the process guides it and gives it meaning. Only when our interaction with the world becomes consciously contemplative can we expect to heal the root cause of our ecological crisis— action deficient in and practically devoid of contemplation.

3. Poiesis, the productive dunamis or power of contemplation. Contemplation is not only the Omega but also the Alpha of action, its matrix. Vision determines action. As you see, so you act. The call to contemplation is not impractical, not a luxury for dreamers, but provides the effective foundation for the practical. Contemplation does not put your head in a cloud, but is what takes it out of a cloud. Contemplative insight, moreover, must constantly be renewed, deepened, lest it be absorbed by routinized action or become structurally outdated or ineffectively narrow.

4. The interpenetration of all in each and each in all realized in Nous, Intellect. This contemplative vision at once reconciles the Deep Ecology principle of equality with the principle of value hierarchization. At the deep, common level of Nous, all are one and all are Nous; but in the more outer levels of phenomenal emanation each can be categorized "according to their nearness to the first principles." Value differentiation can never negate the fundamental insight of equality, however, as well as the ethical principle which flows from it: never treat anything as a means only, for nothing is devoid of intrinsic value.

5. The importance of beauty for human soul-being. Beauty is not merely a luxury or frill, but a necessity of survival. Nature lovers often speak of the soul-stirring or spiritual power of natural beauty. Plotinus contributes towards a philosophical grounding and understanding of it.

6. The importance of eros or love for the realization of goodness. Plotinus argues that love is the self-perfecting nisus of value realization. To insist on the importance of love in an ecological ethic is not merely a gesture to the romantics but is a recognition of its fundamental necessity for any viable ecological ethic.

7. The importance of symbolic knowledge, which is to say, the recognition of other means of knowing besides the cognitive. Plotinus admits of a more integral approach to knowledge involving the imagination, passions, aesthetic and moral sensibilities as well as the rational.

8. Play is a great aid for serious knowledge and for contemplation. This has important implications for moral education.[10]

9. The metaphysical view of time as a dunamis of eternity. There is a divine significance in the unfoldment of time. So also should we see the rhythms of nature as "images of eternity," not merely as mechanical accidents.

10. Contemplation is not only of vital relevance for eco-ethics, but eco-praxis is necessary to contemplation and making manifest the true life. This is, of course, not explicit in Plotinus, but an extrapolation. In the final paragraph of the foregoing section concerning dialectic it was argued that it is not enough to merely think one's way to It, but a more integral effort is required. We interpret this to mean that the whole soul needs to be worked on, which means not just the theoretical and not just the individual

or human parts of the soul, but the whole soul which includes nature. We conclude, therefore, that working on (purifying, perfecting, etc.) the whole soul implies an ecological praxis, a conscientious and insight-honed sensitive relationship with nature.

ALL LIFE IS YOGA

In the effort to overcome our alienated relationship with nature, many ecologically concerned philosophers have made overtures to Asian philosophies.[1] The principal appeal of the major Asian philosophies as represented by Advaita Vedanta, Mahayana Buddhism, and Taoism, is their nondualism. Nondualism is clearly an Asian contribution to the world's set of philosophical worldviews, as Western cultures have very rarely produced a nondual philosophical worldview. Plotinus and possibly Eckhart are perhaps the main representatives of nondualism in the West. Other Western counterparts to nondualism, such as Spinoza, are more technically characterized as pantheistic, whereas none of the major Asian philosophies are pantheistic. Advaita Vedanta, Mahayana Buddhism, and Taoism are rather panentheistic. Panentheism means all is in the divine. This implies that the divine embraces and pervades the entire universe, and at the same time transcends it as the inexhaustible and the unmanifest. The pervasion of the divine or absolute in the phenomenal is not like that of a hand in glove, in which the matter ensouled is a completely unspiritual substance. Rather, the phenomenal is simply the absolute manifested in creation, under the conditions of the many. Things and creatures are not simply and decisively cast out of the absolute into an alien (i.e., nonspiritual) place, but as manifestations of the absolute all things have a depth dimension, at the center or ground of which is the unconditioned absolute.

In panentheistic philosophies the general consensus is that finite expressions of the absolute or spirit are relatively independent substances endowed with a relative measure of freedom, whereas in pantheism finite spirits are modes of the infinite substance and as such have not independent existence and real freedom of their own. Western interpretations of Asian philosophies are frequently pantheistic, but such interpretations could only be derived from certain assertions found in Asian philosophical texts divorced from the philosophy as a whole.

While pantheism attracts some ecologically concerned philosophers, in itself it could as easily supply the ground for a grossly anti-ecological viewpoint. If all value is reducible to the one original substance underlying all phenomenal modes, there is little to justify one arrangement of affairs over any other—all are equally false. Indeed, a perversely anti-ecological policy could conceivable be defended as hastening our return to the truth. Given the deeply imbedded dualism of Western monotheism, pantheism in the West readily lends itself to interpretation along lines of the shadow side of the monotheistic world view, and as such would be a form of Gnosticism.[2] Such a philosophy, whether it is idealistic, scientific, Marxist, or existentialistic, fails to supply an adequate basis for an ecological philosophy because it can only acknowledge some aspects of reality at the expense of others.

While the West could produce, and perhaps already has, a nondual philosophy capable of grounding a convincing ecological ethic without any aid from nonwestern philosophies, there are impelling reasons for believing that Western philosophers do need to lend an ear to nonwestern philosophers to help them out of their dilemma. It was argued previously that crosscultural studies in philosophy will aid the philosopher to approach an integral worldview, and it is the contention of this thesis that only an integral philosophy and ecological ethic is adequate to the task we face today. Secondly, Western philosophers will find in Asian philosophies resources for the construction of a contemporary ecological ethic that will have the force of tradition. That a tradition has existed for some time is, of course, no reason for accepting it, but it can lend some strength to contemporary philosophical expression. Tapping such strength is not only pragmatic but, in a world in which we all share each other's environmental problems, necessary. Unprecedented international cooperation in facing the urgent problems of worldwide environmental degradation is increasingly necessary. Unless such an international and transcultural endeavor is also exercised on the philosophical level, the projects on the technical level will be merely piecemeal and ineffective.[3]

It is for these reasons, and others that will become evident in the exposition to follow, that I choose to draw from the Integral Nondualism of Aurobindo Ghose. Not only is this a case of a Western philosopher enlisting the aid of an Eastern philosopher, but the Eastern philosopher in question is one who has himself already drawn from Western philosophy in order to articulate a modern Vedānta. We are thus in the arena of world philosophy, which is a different matter from the one in which the representative of one hemispheric culture is reporting on what a philosopher of another hemispheric culture thought. In what follows we will be talking more *with* Sri Aurobindo than attempting a scholarly summary *about* his works in Yoga philosophy.[4]

Sri Aurobindo, whose philosophical and multifaceted career spans the first half of the twentieth century, sought to temper the excessively spiritual transcendentalism and illusionism of Advaita Vedanta—a tendency that was exacerbated by the pessimism generated in India by several centuries of colonial rule—with a life- and matter-affirming realism derived from both Western and Indian sources. Since Aurobindo was very reticent in acknowledging his Western sources, we can only say with confidence that he drew on Neoplatonism, Hegelianism (via the Romantic poets), and Bergson. From the latter two Aurobindo was inspired to elevate the concept of time out of the magical and mythic structure with which Indian thought had been largely associated. In Aurobindo's writings history and evolution acquired a significance never before contemplated in Indian philosophy, yet he was able to do so using the language of India's traditions, primarily that of the Tantric tradition of integral, nondual Vedānta.

Just as the Tantric tradition is primarily a Yoga, so is the central thread and intent of Aurobindo's work Yoga. It would be impossible to summarize this intent through all of Aurobindo's writings in various fields, or even to outline his philosophical system adequately here. I will rather focus on some of the philosophical implications of his Integral *(Purna)* Yoga that are especially relevant to the search for an ecological ethic.

In *The Synthesis of Yoga*, Aurobindo states that all life is Yoga, by which he means that all forms of life can be characterized as conscious or subconscious intentional processes striving to actualize a divinized existence. Yoga describes the telos of all things; it is

> a methodised effort towards self-perfection by the expression of the potentialities latent in the being and a union of the human individual with the universal and transcendent Existence we see partially expressed in man and in the Cosmos. But all life, when we look behind its appearances, is a vast Yoga of Nature attempting to realise her perfection in an ever increasing expression of her potentialities and to unite herself with her own divine reality.[5]

We may recall here that Plotinus similarly extended the application of what is conventionally understood as a human sensitivity, contemplation, to all of nature. For Aurobindo what has come to be designated as Yoga is the self-conscious intensification of the natural world process. This self-conscious intensification generally is systematized into a school of Yoga. Any given system of yoga, says Aurobindo,

> can be no more than a selection or a compression, into narrower but more energetic forms of intensity, of the general methods which are already being used loosely, largely, in a leisurely movement, with a profuser apparent waste of material and energy but a more complete combination by the great Mother in her vast upward labour.[6]

This organic conception of Yoga may come as a surprise to those who understand it to be a method of mystical escape from the phenomenal world of suffering. Aurobindo, however, views such world-fleeing Yoga as an excess, or lopsided development that achieves certain spiritual attainments at the cost of an impoverished outer life. Inner freedom, however, need not be paid for by an outer death. This false assumption, all the more vicious because partially true, is the principal cause of India's social stagnation, Aurobindo contends. It is, however, a conception of Yoga that is based on a false, because partial, understanding of nature. It is manifestly true that embodied life presents an obstacle to the realization of a spiritual life.

But ontologizing this difficulty into an absolute commits one to a category mistake, namely of making a relative opposition within the one movement of nature into a de facto absolute duality of two substances, eventhough, de jure, one contends that the lower of the two substances is not real. Aurobindo compares this one-sided spiritual development with one-sided technological development:

> But as in physical knowledge the multiplication of scientific processes has its disadvantages, as that tends, for instance, to develop a victorious artificiality which overwhelms our natural human life under a load of machinery and to purchase certain forms of freedom and mastery at the price of an increased servitude . . . .[7]

At the risk of being charged with oversimplification, it can be said that East and West represent respectively cultural choices in favor of one side of the great duality, the one for spiritual development, the other for physical. Neither can achieve a healthy perfection, which is to say, harmonious and integral actualization of human potential. Hence there is some irony in the call for westernization among Asians and a corresponding looking to the East for a remedy to the problems of contemporary Western civilization. Unless such importation is undertaken with the intention of achieving a more harmonious balance, one can only expect to trade one set of problems for another.

For an organic conception of Yoga to be more than a redundant synonym for the process of nature, it is to convey something about the latter which is usually not noticed. That is indeed what Yoga intends: "a plunge into all the profundities of soul,"[8] where soul is the involved divinity supporting all individual existence in nature. This "plunge" involves an epistemological shift allowing for an enriched ontological experience, bringing into play depth energies and dimensions of consciousness not usually noticed or even suspected at the surface level of conventional consciousness. "Bringing into play" is not a mere turn of phrase in this case, but expresses the underlying philosophical concept of *līla*, or divine play.

Līla is the dynamic enactment of Brahman conceived as *saccidānanda*. While Brahman in itself transcends the grasp of human experience, mystical experience can nevertheless discover the nature of Brahman in identity with it.[9] Saccidānanda, according to the Vedāntic tradition, is the most adequate equation conceivable within the limits of thought and language. The Sanskrit term is an adjectival compound composed of *sat*, "being, existence," *cit*, "consciousness" (and, according to Aurobindo and the Tantric tradition, "will" or "force", hence often referred to as *cit-shakti*, "consciousness-force"), and *ānanda*, "blissful." These descriptive terms serve as the basis for a three-fold schema of divine causality: sat being the material cause, cit the efficient, and ānanda the teleological. What Aurobindo calls the involution of saccidānanda into creation is the play of the divine characterizable as sat being involuted by cit for the sake of ānanda.

This characterization of divine creation as līla has several advantageous features over more "serious" attempts to explain the universe. For one, it puts in parentheses, as it were, the tendency to literalness of terms which more serious theologizing falls prey to. Linguistic signs are like two-dimensional attempts to portray a three-dimensional situation: they are useful so long as one does not confuse the territory with the map. This caution applies a fortiori when language that is inherently dualistic is used to say something about nondual reality. Otherwise one would be misled to think, for example, of nondual reality as reality distinct from unreality, of nondual consciousness as distinct from unconsciousness, and of ānanda as blissfulness that is different or in opposition to phenomenal suffering. Such a dualistic understanding of saccidānanda is a complete misunderstanding of the concept for it fails to compensate the relativeness of mental "place" with an unbounded intuition of the arelational which grounds it, as it were (i.e., where "ground" is also not to be taken with metaphysical literalness). Neither are the terms of the trinity to be understood as different parts or persons as in the Christian trinity, their distinctions being a mental one.

Another advantage to the concept of creation as play involves the essential identity of means and end. Just as play is done for the sake of play, all other considerations being secondary, so is the process of divine creation undergone for the sake of ānanda, which is its own nature. Hence divine play is a self-sufficient explanation of creation which need not be burdened with our projections of extrinsic purposiveness. Brahman, says Aurobindo in support of the Vedāntic conception, is absolutely self-sufficient and therefore has no need to create. Creation is a play Brahman engages in out of the exhuberant fulness of its blissful nature. And since the universe is the divine play, all things essentially partake of this playful nature. Which is to say that divine joy is not primarily something to strive for but is already present in nature however involuted and dormant it may seem to be.[10]

That this conception of creation as divine play may be found attractive to ecological philosophers and lovers of nature should surprise no one. Much of our environmental problems are the direct result of striving for extrinsic goods. Extending or applying the concept of play to culture, we find, on the one hand, that end-oriented societies turn play into a game in which the object is to win; in such a society one can not be happy unless one is successful. In a means-oriented society, on the other hand, the game is a sort of purposeless play; in such a society, if one is happy, then one is successful. Humanity need not transform the earth into a garbage dump in order to be happy. Human society, clearly, must become more means-oriented if it is to survive.[11]

To become means-oriented, however, is not sufficiently specific. Play, particularly in the phenomenal world of diversity, involves the interaction of many different forces, allowing for many different emphases or types of games, in the broadest sense of the word. Since play at the transcendental level is practically inscrutable,[12] the form play (i.e., way of being) takes in the phenomenal world is subject to hermeneutical judgement.

Aurobindo states that although at its transcendental origin the divine līla is indeterminate and absolutely free, once it precipitates into a freely chosen creative process, a determinate structure comes into play. With this determinate structure purposiveness also comes into play. It comes *into* play, which is to say that the transcendental origin of complete freedom and unbounded bliss always remains the ultimate context of ontological and evolutionary developments. Purposiveness is, therefore, also part of the līla. Consequently, exclusive emphasis on the purposelessness of divine and, subsequently, world play entails a confusion of noumenal and phenomenal levels, the converse of Kant's transcendental fallacy, namely, attributing to the phenomenal sphere what properly belongs to the noumenal.

Hence, concerning the 'why' of divine creation, something can be said about it that is more than mere tautology. Ānanda is both means and end, but this does not require that end and means be identical in every respect. To posit complete identity of end and means, Aurobindo goes so far to say, infers the absurdity of creation. The view that maintains Brahman's creation of an absurd universe is self-contradictory, for it entails the supposition that it was created by Ignorance, by a Schopenhauerian Blind Will. This, yet another version of the Gnostic worldview, fails for reasons similar to the fallacy of naturalistic world views, namely the inability to account for order, reason, values, spirit, freedom, hope, evolution, and teleology.

That Indian cosmologies never went to the extreme view of Gnosticism, which posits the creation of the world to be the work of an evil or ignorant demiurge, is in part due to their relative lack of preoccupation with the fate of the universe or even cosmology in general. Indian philosophy has been predominantly concerned with the destiny of the individual. The cosmos was, for all practical purposes, nothing more than an elaborate stage on which the individual performed the drama of self-liberation, upon attainment of which the cosmos would supposedly cease to exist for him. The nature of liberated existence, that is, whether it was individual or not, differed among the schools, but there was hardly any disagreement over the fate of the universe: it is doomed to a perpetual cycle of birth, evolution and dissolution. Hence the existential or objective aspect of reality did not merit the philosopher's interest except as a vehicle of value. The Indian philosopher was primarily interested in the axiological aspect of reality, for without value a thing had no reality as such. Philosophy, therefore, emphasized the practical rather than the theoretical, for the quintessential problem was the individual's quest for value.[13]

The supreme value is saccidānanda. In it existence and value (sat and cit) are identical, which is optimal felicity (ānanda). Its unfolding play through the world of phenomena is what constitutes their value, and they are graded according to the quality of ānanda which manifests in them. Hence the axiological hierarchy of matter, life, mind, spirit.

Aurobindo criticizes the narrowly axiological emphasis of the Indian traditions with their one-sided preoccupation with individual salvation. The mythological structure of consciousness in which this cyclical and dipolar worldview was meaningful has witnessed the predominance of place given to the mental structure and its scientific worldview, largely under impetus of Western colonialism. The delegitimated cyclical world view could only appear meaningless to the intellect sharpened by this psychohistorical transformation. A new synthesis of the axiological insights of Indian philosophy and the scientific orientation of Western philosophy was called for and which Aurobindo provided with his philosophy of the divine evolution of consciousness.

Evolution, Aurobindo argues, can only be accounted for by a prior involution of the saccidānanda in matter. In the process of involution the unity of saccidānanda is fragmented into multiplicity, each unit of which is an embryonic soul which begins its evolutionary ascent. The ascent is one of increasing liberation or self-manifestation of the divine. Aurobindo agrees with the general intent of the Indian tradition that the objective world of phenomena assumes value (or actualizes value) only as it has a relation to the soul, for it serves as the foundation for evolution, which is teleologically spiritual. Nature is a field, an occasion or means for the soul's progression in time, the soul's scaffolding. But nature is not just a stepping stone for the soul, for each ascent of the soul occasions a reversal of consciousness in which the foundation of ascent is integrated with the new evolutionary attainment. Inorganic matter becomes in turn organic, vegetative, sensitive and, in man, the thinking brain.[14]

The mechanism of the evolutionary ascent is rebirth of the individual soul into increasingly complex bodies. As a power of saccidānanda the soul's individuality is phenomenal, but Aurobindo insists that this individuality is neither illusory nor ephemeral: if it were, cosmic creation and evolution would be a purely meaningless and unnecessary līla. In his schema, the individual assumes real significance, and is a stance of Brahman as much as the transcendental and the cosmic. It is precisely in the sphere of phenomenal individuality that evolution becomes actualized and meaningful. A pantheistic conception of evolution could be actual, but would be meaningless. A conception of real individuals as the subjects of evolution preserves at once the pantheistic notion of the one Self of all, Ātman or saccidānanda, as the inner ground of subjectivity and a real phenomenal concentration of the spirit as one which out of almost complete suppression in matter progressively manifests the powers of spirit in a long series of reincarnations (of which a relatively long series of human births form the middle term) which aims to fulfill itself in perfect unity-in-diversity representing a real advance over primal undifferentiated unity.[15]

A real end, with benefit to real individuals makes Aurobindo's conception of evolution a meaningful one. The individuals concerned, moreover, are not only human but all living things. Since all living things have a common origin, which they each retain as their underlying self, and a similar destiny, there exists a certain equality among all living things. This more or less timeless equality is obscured in the temporal order of things. So humans are presently first among equals, for in them the evolving spirit has become reflectively self-conscious. In man the evolutionary process becomes conscious. Though humans are at the forefront of evolution, they are not its end and limit, at least not as presently constituted. However, since humans are self-conscious and can consciously take up the work of evolution (i.e., Yoga), further evolutionary progress is possible in the human species. Aurobindo is so convinced of the necessity and inevitability of further evolution towards what he calls the supramenta that should humans not take up the task of conscious evolution then the evolutionary nisus in nature will bypass them and create a new species who will be to man as man is to animals.[16]

In contradistinction to those of the traditional Yogas whose aim it was to transcend and become free of the realm of nature, Aurobindo's Integral Yoga aims at a dynamic self-identification with the creative impetus in nature, conceived in theistic terms as the Divine Mother who ultimately controls the process of evolution which embodies her physical form. Haridas Chaudhuri, an interpreter of Aurobindo's philosophy, has variously described the goal of Integral Yoga as "the out flowering of the Divine in collective humanity," "liberation *in* and *of* Nature, and not simply *from* Nature," "spiritual self-manifestation as distinguished from mere self-realization."[17]

Just as those magico-mythic dualistic worldviews had yogic systems of self-culture or liberative ascent from the world that corresponded to those views, so is Aurobindo's view of an integral evolutionary nondualism realized in a Yoga that complements the ascent of the individual consciousness with the descent of the supramental founts of consciousness. Aurobindo boasts that his Yoga begins where all other Yogas end, for in his system personal liberation or enlightenment is not the end but a means of spiritualizing the world. Spiritualizing the world is a continuation of the evolutionary project of incarnating saccidānanda, only, with the advent of Integral Yoga, this process, it is purported, will be speeded up and intensified beyond what has heretofore been possible.

The dialectic of evolution is one of ascent followed by integration. Accepting evolution as the will of the divine, Integral Yoga gives expression to this will by supplementing the negation of ascent by a deeper and fuller affirmation (which constitutes the movement of descent). The negation (of "the world" or conventional consciousness) required by or implied in ascent or the mystical absorption of consciousness is for Aurobindo merely instrumental, for the higher that one can rise the more one can bring down or be a conduit for divine power into the mental, vital, and physical levels of consciousness. The degree to which a Yogi has actualized the yogic process of ascent and descent are identified as the stages of psychicization, spiritualization, and supramentalization.[18]

The realization of the supermind will inaugurate a great new era in terrestial evolution, Aurobindo believes. It is a level of consciousness not previously achieved in the long traditions of Yoga and mysticism whose spiritual attainments, though lofty and important, have not served to change human nature to any significant extent or to overcome its evil tendencies during the course of their operative existence for the past three millenia. The supramental descent, however, will bring with it an irresistable power of transformation which will spiritualize not only human nature but the world as a whole.

AUROBINDO'S YOGA AND PLOTINUS'S CONTEMPLATION

Both Aurobindo and Plotinus expound metaphysical views characterizable as qualified monism. Human life is a microcosmic expression of macrocosmic life and becomes fully authentic when it becomes self-consciously contemplative. In both of these views all living beings have their origin in the Absolute and, consciously or not, aspire to return to it. The return to the Absolute is effected by contemplation in Plotinus and by Yoga in Aurobindo, and both of these praxes involve a dialectic of consciousness encompassing "ascent" and "descent". Ascent and descent can be interpreted along either metaphysical or contemplative lines. In terms of the dynamics of contemplation or Yoga, Plotinus' and Aurobindo's use of ascent and descent and theoria and poiesis are very similar.

The metaphysical expositions have important differences, however, particularly in the significance of ascent. For Plotinus the return or ascent is to the point of origin. He is ambivalent as to whether this involves a complete absorption of the individual in the One or whether the individual enjoys a blessed status in the unity-in-diversity of Nous. The temporal interlude between Alpha and Omega is conceived of in purely mythic terms, being the lower member of the eternity/time polarity. There is nothing that it can contribute to the individual's eternal and noumenal status. Nevertheless, Plotinus does not on that account wish to go so far as the Gnostics who condemn the phenomenal world of nature as in itself evil. Nature is good because it participates in the Forms and bad insofar as its participation is weak. We have seen that though Plotinus clearly explains the tolmaic or affirmative and creative poiesis of the contemplative life, he is so overpredominantly concerned with the negative return movement of consciousness that he is completely negligent in regards to the possibility that the enlightened sage may have important work to do in the world for which his or her visions of the intelligibles and of the One were as much means as end. The world is thus left dangling in ambivalence, for Plotinus is unable to break out of the circular, mythic view of time inherited from Plato. Such a breakthrough had to wait another two centuries for Augustine's philosophy of history.

However much such a schema is faithful to the experience of contemplative ascent, it cannot satisfy our need for meaning. Both the processional descent and ascent are meaningful, but in Plotinus' system these cancel each other out. What point descent when the return is to the point of origin? What point the ascent when descent will necessarily follow? In Aurobindo's involution-evolutionary schema the whole universal process becomes meaningful because it breaks out of the futile circle and allows ascent and descent to complement each other. In the integral structure evolution is neither circular nor linear but something more like a spiral. In order to maximize value in the phenomenal world, the Yogi must tap its source in the noumenal through the ascent of consciousness. The ascent becomes meaningful because it is no longer the path of individual escape out of time to an extratemporal bliss. The individual, rather, deepens his or her participation in the universal līla, which is also a universal or collective Yoga, by transcending the outmoded psycho-temporal strictures of a mental-structured consciousness and attaining the time-freedom or mastery of time characteristic of the integral structure of consciousness.

In a universal Yoga the extent of an individual's evolutionary progress is more or less conditioned and limited by the overall evolution of the world (from which it is not separate), particularly the human race because of its pivotal significance and responsibility for the evolution of consciousness. Hence the individual has a real stake in the well-being of the world and its inhabitants. Given the reincarnational schema, furthermore, it is not a responsibility one can escape from whether via death or via liberation or redemption, for however transitory the embodied personality, its true self is immortal and must seek to incarnate itself in the conditions provided for it by previous incarnations in order to satisfy its nisus for evolutionary perfection, one in which maximum individual freedom is in perfect harmony with the collectivity of all beings.

Because Integral Yoga is the self-conscious apex of the world Yoga it cannot but be a praxis of ecological participation.[19] Hence an integral Yoga is an eco-yoga or must become so to realize its integrality. But this eco-yoga is not merely a magical Yoga for maintaining homeostatic ecological harmony, for it is also the self-conscious expression of the evolutionary nisus for the realization/ creation of new values. Achieving a balance between these contrary tendencies is something an integral Yoga is equipped to do for it is itself a balance between play (the joyful contentment with the being of things as they are) and seriousness (purposive evolutionary endeavor or *sādhana*).

Environmental ethics is the attempt to correct a deficient ethics, to make it more fully moral. In this regard it could be claimed that only an integral eco-yoga would be fully moral (i.e., as moral as is possible for this day and age, and where moral is not merely a mental-rational category) because it is a synthesis (or more properly, a "synairesis" according to Gebser)[20] of the moral values of all the structures of consciousness. It would incorporate the full magical sympathy of Deep Ecology, the imaginative play and love (of polarized differences) of the mythic, and the "appropriate" eco-evolutionary *techne* of the mental-rational.[21]

TOWARDS AN INTEGRAL ECOLOGICAL ETHIC

In our survey of contemporary approaches to environmental ethics it was argued that those approaches were not adequate because not integral, or not sufficiently integral as in the case of Skolimowski's eco-philosophy. The premise on which our judgement is based is that there is an evolution of consciousness during which development several distinguishable structures were actualized. The psychosocial predominance of a newly actualized structure over the others constitutes a characteristic psychohistorical era, but the influence of each of the structures (which we have taken with Gebser to be the archaic, the magical, the mythic, the mental-rational, and the integral) is not limited to the era in which it is predominant. We agree with Gebser that the era of the mental structure is currently in its rational, waning phase. During this phase a psychohistorical structure's "immune system" is increasingly unable to ward off deficient ideologies. This same weakness is apparently a necessary precondition for the emergence of a new structure of consciousness, such as the integral one today appearing with greater frequency on the edges of the rational structure. Assuming that only an integral metaphysic and worldview would be adequate for an ecological ethic for this transitional period toward the integral era, the main task of this essay is to provide a means or guide to help judge which philosophical endeavors are in step with the emerging world view and its requirements and which are not.

The greatest obstacle in the way of presenting an integral worldview lies in the built-in mental bias of contemporary philosophical discourse on the one hand and of its traditionalist alternatives on the other. The task of presenting an integral philosophy is not hopeless, however, because it is not non-existent; it does not have to be invented de novo. Expressions of an integral nature are found sprinkled throughout the literature of the mental era and even in those of the mythic (the Vedas, for example). We have presented Plotinus and Sri Aurobindo as representatives of the integral structure of consciousness, the latter more fully so than the former. Neither of these philosophers have served in the theoretical forays of ecological philosophers, yet their insights and metaphysical frameworks are, I believe, of vital relevance to the urgent task of shaping a viable ecological ethic. This final chapter will attempt to further explicate this claim.

We have heard from many ecologically concerned philosophers that the most serious obstacle in the way of an environmental ethic is the anthropocentrism of modern culture. Skolimowski countered that the problem is not anthropocentrism as such, which is unavoidable for humans, but the quality of anthropocentrism, namely whether it is benevolent or vicious ecologically. The nature of this controversy could perhaps be resolved by a different use of terms. If we use the term "egocentric" instead of "anthropocentric" and then identify the egocentric nature of our dominant worldview, I believe it would be easier to arrive at a consensus among ecological philosophers. This shift of emphasis towards a more psychological term helps to underscore the personal transformation required to bring an integral ecological ethic into being; much more is called for than a changed theoretical orientation.[1]

The transformation of practical life from the egocentric to an ecocentric one is much more likely to be invoked by an opening of the heart than by an intellectual opening of the mind alone. The practical transformation would, of course, be even more likely if the opening involved both heart and mind. Indeed, this is what an integral ethic requires. In the integral structure of consciousness the privileged status appropriated by the intellectual (mental) gives way to an essential equality of consciousness structures or powers, harmonized or integrated by the actualized insight-power (cit-shakti) of the integral consciousness.

The reason why intellectual insight often has no effect on practical life is that the insight is of value essences which are merely potential in the conscience of the moral agent. It is feeling which actualizes them. Our primary relations to the world, the outer world of things, the intersubjective world of others and the inner world of self, are primarily emotional and only secondarily conceptual; and it is this emotional or feeling relationship that is value-realizing. The contemporary crisis in morals is not due so much to the conceptual figuration of the mental structure as to its suppression of the feelings and passions associated with the magical and mythic psychohistorical structures. This suppression is not total in scope, obviously, but one of procrustean limitation, such that feelings and passions are only allowed to realize the lowest values, those of pleasure and utility. The realization of higher, nonutilitarian values is reduced in significance to mere subjective ("emotive") feeling and, as such, in the same category of pleasure and utility values. Actively cultivating the higher feelings and passions to realize values higher than the utilitarian or subjective ones would contradict the mental-rational dogma of nature's value-neutrality.

This raises the question whether the contemporary crisis in values, as Skolimowski calls it, is a result of a materialist metaphysics or of the desublimation of feeling. If it is a case of the latter, then a new metaphysics would not change the picture much. From an integral perspective, however, the relationship between feeling and metaphysics (or, more broadly, worldview) is not asymmetrically transitive but mutual or symbiotic: they influence each other. Each may lead the other towards the realization of value, depending on circumstances. The cultivation of feeling discovers new values, inspiring reason to formulate a new understanding. Or reason may rebel against prevalent narrowness of feeling and through its power of critique agitate and inspire the passions to bring about a new order of relationship. Value-realizing feelings which fail to articulate the logos or essence and significance of the new values can provide no enduring norms for the guidance and benefit of society.

Though feeling and reason are mutually dependent, there are

practical advantages for stressing the priority of feeling in moral education. Max Scheler argued for this priority of feeling in his *Formalism in Ethics and Non-Formal Ethics of Values*. It is primarily the feelings which realize value and bear persons up in moral development. The higher feelings, of which love is the quintessential, enable the bearer to see more of what is present, that is, more than what is empirically given. This seeing of the rich possibilities of value in what is loved helps the love object to actualize these values.[2]

Although I agree with Scheler, especially in the case of the higher feelings such as love, it is also true that feelings can be the obstacle to greater moral sensitivity. Scheler was quite aware of this, too, as his unparalleled analysis of resentment makes clear. Both feelings and reason can be either open or closed, progressive or regressive, in regards to moral and overall human development. Hence, rather than attempting to determine which of these is primary or more fundamental, I think it would be more helpful for purposes of moral development to understand both reason and feeling as modes of contemplation. Here we take inspiration from Plotinus and Aurobindo, both of whom take contemplation (or Yoga) as a characterization of the fundamental process of nature, most intensely manifested in humans.

This position, that all nature contemplates, is also known as panpsychism. This is basically the philosophical ground that Deep Ecologists say is required in order to found a biocentric ecological ethic. Panpsychism can be arrived at through reason and through the aesthetical disclosures of feeling, but much more fundamentally it is a revelation of gnosis or contemplation. There is, of course, a circularity involved in this assertion. This is unavoidable, for the revelation obtained in gnosis is self-revelation, a revelation of universal self. As such it involves a particular kind of seeing or epistemic intuition, indeed the highest or fullest measure of seeing or knowing possible for human persons. What is being asserted is all of reality, or nature (as in the Greek sense of *phusis*) in its wholeness, including those levels of nature unseen and unknown by science and its philosophical apologists. It is an intuition of identity or oneness.

It is not only environmental ethics which requires the recognition of nature in its wholeness, but morality as such. Modern forms of ethics which appeal to the scientific worldview cannot, from the holistic perspective, be truly moral. Moral judgements employing scientific reasoning are depending on an ideal of knowledge that is itself based on *ressentiment* valuation, Max Scheler argues.[3] Resentment (the English word does not capture the richly nuanced meaning of the French ressentiment), according to Nietzsche, is the slavish reaction to master morality, where master morality requires a cultivated competence, hence, of the elite or masters. In order to mask its guilt over its moral incompetence or inferiority, the herd mentality replaces the master morality by a more democratic or scientific one. Thus, whereas traditional morality upheld the moral ideal of ego-transcendence, modern morality is egocentric. Egoism, a practice of moral deficiency, through resentment, becomes formalized in scientific theory, which in turn legitimizes an egocentric practice. Hence the moral bankruptcy of scientistic morality, according to Scheler. Ecological ethics is radical only in the sense that it rejects egocentric morality based on ressentiment and insists on morality, which must be nonegocentric and holistic. Contemplation, broadly conceived, is the route by which one moves from egocentricity to ecocentricity in ethics.

An alternative to playing the prophet denouncing modern morality as immoral is the Taoist approach.[4] Rather than trying to reform morality, Lao Tzu and his followers held that "morality" is part of the problem—another expression of humanistic hubris by which man places himself above nature, thereby unwittingly cutting himself off from harmony with nature or Tao. There "harmony with the Tao," or the living realization of panpsychism, replaces morality. Heidegger makes a parallel move in regards to metaphysics. So also some ecological philosophers resent having their thought categorized as environmental ethics: environmental ethics, as "applied ethics," is loaded with presuppositions that are part of the problem.[5]

I see no unresolvable contradiction between rejection of "morality" and establishing the ideal of an integral ethic, just as I see no contradiction between agreeing with Heidegger's project to deconstruct metaphysics and engaging in speculative thought with a new sensitivity about its purpose that the deconstruction allowed or liberated. The contradiction is overcome in the integral synthesis, for integral ethics and integral metaphysics are not ethics and metaphysics as characterized by the mental-rational structure. It is not a mental-rational synthesis, but one that integrates instinct, emotion, feeling, imagination, and reason through contemplative intuition. Neither does the integral understanding confront the present crisis with a call of "back to religion" or "back to magical paganism." It is rather one which stems from a creative vision, creative in the sense that it reaches beyond time-worn values and apprehends new values.

These values are transcendent, in that they transcend the psycho-temporal structures of consciousness characterized as magical, mythic, and mental. But they are not altogether transcendent, for they are apprehended in nature and seek creative embodiment in cultural life. Integral realization of value in life is effected through recruiting the cognitive and volitional powers of the passions, the imagination and the intellect so that one's involvement in nature is not just along one line or another but one with full, multidimensional participation, which alone can bring into play the full range of values potential in nature.

The apprehension of new, higher values in nature, the gnosis of an integral vision, the realization and embodiment of an ecological moral sensibility, are the theoria and poiesis, the inward and outward dynamics, of contemplation. These are not so much the ingredients that make up contemplation as the expressions of healthy and unfettered contemplation, evolved contemplation. Hence in the integral structure it is contemplation as a whole, of the whole, and as the life of the whole, which must be emphasized over the particular expressions to which it has given birth. It must further be emphasized that the ideal of integral contemplation is not the steady-state equilibrium of the magical and mythic structures, nor the linear progress of a will-to-power as in the mental structure, but of a dynamic whole realizing itself in progressive diversifying integrations. Contemplative expressions which fall short of the integral vision can be judged from this perspective of greatest wholeness as products of weak contemplation, and may properly be regarded as pathological (deficient *pathos*). In this schema of evolutionary contemplation there will always be forms of contemplation resistant to change and greater integration, precisely the forms which creative contemplation must transcend and transform into efficient forms.[6]

An objection against the relevance of contemplation for purposes of establishing a viable ecological ethic might look like this: either contemplation is a talent which so few can cultivate to an adequate degree that its requirement as the basis for an ecological ethic would ensure that such an ethic will never take hold for human society generally; or contemplation is so general (all nature contemplates) that it merely describes what everyone is already doing and so changes nothing.

What this objection overlooks is that there is a vast continuum of degrees of contemplation and that in the human spectrum contemplation can be strong or weak, better or worse, and, furthermore, that the higher or better contemplations exert proportionally a much greater influence on the lower or weaker contemplations than vice versa. It is only when the higher contemplations are weak or in a waning phase that the lower contemplations characterized by egoistic desire appear to have greater (repressive) influence over the higher.[7] The key to containing the disharmonizing forces of egoism (including collective egoism or anthropocentrism and its devastating effects on the environment) is not the imposition of repressive ego-restraining measures, but the cultivation of higher contemplations. Of course, some restraint on egoistic excess and exploitation may be necessary in order to divert sufficient energy to contemplation and more balanced ways of living.

A contemporary parallel to the idea of advancing degrees of contemplation is found in Michael Polanyi's theory of knowledge which he calls Personal Knowledge. Building on the Gestalt concept of the background/foreground or the field/focussing aspects of perception and understanding, Polanyi describes how the field, or tacit dimension, orients and integrates the focal objects of awareness. Their joint operation results in meaningful apprehension. This is, of course, a Kantian conception of knowledge, only for Polanyi the theoretical component includes more than categories of understanding. The theoretical, field or tacit dimension is more personal, involving feelings, expectations, hope, sense of responsibility, and interest. All of these factors contribute to the ordering of facts into a meaningful whole, and the deployment of these factors for understanding constitutes a personal indwelling in the object. Since personal indwelling is a necessary ingredient for any type of knowledge the ideal of objective knowledge is an unattainable myth. Personal indwelling is one way to describe the function of contemplation, for contemplation seeks to know things as fully as possible, intuiting their *logoi* and ultimately their oneness, which is to say, to indwell it completely. Hence all knowledge is contemplative, at least minimally.[8]

In *The Study of Man*, Polanyi outlines a schema of knowledge disciplines according to their degree of personal indwelling involved, from the least to the greatest. The least degree of personal indwelling in the object of study is exercised in the study of matter; yet even in this case the scientist pursues knowledge motivated by interests and commitment to the conviction that there is something there to be discovered. As such, the knowledge of the object is affected not only by subjectivity, in a Kantian sense, but involves the personality of the one who holds it. The discoverer is filled with a compelling sense of responsibility for the pursuit of a hidden truth which demands his or her service for revealing it. The sciences that study vegetative and animal life respectively involve greater degrees of indwelling on the part of the researcher on account of their greater proximity to human being (there is more of the observer in the observed). When the object of study is human beings then the observer and object are on the same level. Whereas in the sciences of nonhuman objects the observer's subjective, personal and theoretical components of the tacit dimension looked down on the focal objects, in the human sciences the tacit and focal dimensions are on the same level and confused. Here the relationship between knower and known "has definitely lost the character of an observation and has become an encounter instead."[9]

The progression of personal knowledge passes on to its final stage, says Polanyi, when we study great historical personages. When we study heroes we are no longer looking down but up to our subject and educating ourselves in its image.

> To contemplate a person as an ideal is to submit to his authority. The admirer of Napoleon does not judge him by independent previously established standards, but accepts, on the contrary, the figure of Napoleon as a standard for judging himself. Such an admirer may be mistaken in the choice of his hero, but his relation to greatness is correct. We need reverence to perceive greatness, even as we need a telescope to observe spiral nebulae.[10]

Polanyi's praise for "reverent submission to greatness" as the ultimate member of the series of studies is very similar to the Neoplatonic concept of theoria, contemplation. In both cases there is a looking up to something greater, resulting in a participation in the archetype which molds one's character and creative action, poiesis. The concepts are more than merely analogous, for the central importance of exemplars is stressed in most contemplative traditions. The higher reaches of contemplation, the attainment of which are too difficult for most people, are mediated and made more accessible through the living influence of sages and saints. Max Scheler argues that love of an exemplar (model person) is more powerful and more effective than moral laws and norms for molding character: "There can be no reverence for a norm or a moral law that is not founded in reverence for the *person* who posits it—founded ultimately in love for this person as a model."[11] Scheler's emphasis on the model person is directly opposite to Kant's emphasis on the moral law:

> Imitation has no place at all in moral matters. And examples serve only for encouragement, that is, they put beyond doubt the feasibility of what the law commands and they make visible what the practical rule expresses more generally. But examples can never justify us in setting aside their true original, which lies in reason, and letting ourselves be guided by them. (*Grounding for the Metaphysics of Morals*, II.409)

Scheler locates the "highest sense of all moral acts" in a solidaristic realm of best persons, where persons are not merely bearers of acts of reason, but individuals and concrete act-centers of self-value. Moral norms are not good or evil in themselves, but according to whether they ultimately advance or hinder persons to become good. And whether or not the positing of a norm is good depends on the goodness of the person positing. "Nothing on earth allows a person to become good so originally and immediately and necessarily as the evidential and adequate intuition [*Anschauung*] of a good person *in* his goodness."[12] This intuition is not one of information, of specifically good acts, for example, but of goodness which as value or logos can be known not objectively (which is devoid of value) but subjectively by identity or by some sympathetic feeling/intuition approaching identity. Hence, to actually perceive a good person (i.e., to see his or her goodness) is to be transformed morally, to grow into the exemplar. Scheler emphasizes that this transformation takes place in the *being* of the person rather than in volition and acting, and it is the moral being thus transformed which determines volition and acts. The person remains autonomous in his willing; simple imitation or obedience is not the moral transformation being described here. ". . . We learn to will and do *as* the model wills and does, not *what* he wills and does."[13] Models enable us to discover and develop our own person.

Contrary to Polanyi who advises us to choose carefully between authorities, Scheler holds that we do not choose a model. One is rather invited, attracted and captivated by it.[14] Perhaps the difference in opinion can be accounted for by Scheler's phenomenological approach, which bases itself on description rather than explanation. I think he is correct insofar as no model can be effective unless it does attract and, in that sense, being attracted and captivated by a model is primary. The primacy of attraction may claim some support from the phenomenon of falling in love: one does not choose to be in love but falls in love, perhaps even in despite of one's will. But this phenomenon may be culturally conditioned, for in those cultures where marriages are arranged, love follows choice if at all. Furthermore, attraction does not necessarily dictate choice, for one can choose not to follow the whims of attraction. So Polanyi is right: we can and must exercise discrimination and choice in regards to our models. Synthesizing his assertion with Scheler's we could say that we should allow ourselves to be attracted to the most worthy models. Cultivating character requires a proper balance of will and surrender.

The role of model persons in the cultivation of ethical responsibility in society is thus of crucial importance. That Scheler placed so much emphasis on them in his ethical philosophy is understandable given his personalistic perspective. Need we accept personalism in order to emphasize the central role of model persons, let us say ecologically concerned contemplatives, in an ethics based on contemplation? That is, is integral ecological ethics necessarily personalistic? The answer to this question depends on one's definition of personalism.

Classical personalist idealism as represented by Borden Parker Bowne and Edgar Brightman, for example, is a form of enriched Cartesian dualism. Descartes' mental substance is enriched to include qualities other than reason, such as willing and feeling, which contribute to the mature self of well developed human consciousness. The Cartesian material substance is retained virtually unchanged.[15] Such a view of nature is clearly an anthropocentric one wherein nature is devoid of intrinsic value, being merely instrumental for human purposes. Such a view of nature is antithetical to our view that all nature contemplates, a monistic and panpsychist view. Hence, though the importance of model persons remains practically valid, the personalism on which it is based is rejected.

The definition of personhood, however, can be broadened, perhaps even so broad as to coincide with our concept of contemplation, in which case it would constitute a great help towards the recognition of nature's intrinsic worth and moral significance rather than it being a conceptual hindrance. This is made possible through the recognition of degrees of personhood, which Brightman himself admitted, although he himself had not followed it through to its logical conclusion: ". . . Personalism provides for a great variety of quasi-personal substances, from the lowest possible self, to elementary persons, to higher but still fragmented persons, up to the only fully personal substance, God."[16] Frederick Ferre argues that when the human person is recognized to be an imperfect person and yet worthy of dignity, then "it clearly is no barrier to the dignity (or self-worth) of *other* entities that they, too, suffer deficiencies in unity, continuity, or complexity."[17] He thinks that the boundaries of Personalism are flexible enough to include the flora and fauna, and even the physical energy-matter system of the natural order itself.

John Lavely argues that personalistic idealism is a perfectly adequate basis on which to establish the dignity of nature, even if it has not, for the most part, delivered on its principles. "Personalism," he claims, "is the metaphysical hypothesis that there are no non-personal beings."[18] That means the realms of nature and personal being coincide. Lavely reads personalism as a form of panpsychism which holds that there are no properties which are not properties of persons or person-like beings. "And if values are in, of, for such beings, then there are no *purely* instrumental values, for that would be to treat some person or complex of persons (in this case, those whose existence is integrally identified with what we call nature) as an "it", as "things", as *mere* phenomena, as purely instrumental."[19]

The problems of the environment for which the instrumental-ization of values are responsible, are based on the assumption that only humans are persons and all things are instrumental for human purposes. But once the personhood of all things is acknowledged then the dualism of instrumental value and inherent value can no longer be maintained. All are mutually instrumental as well as intrinsically valuable. Lavely concludes that entities are not therefore purely instrumental but are instrumental in virtue of their intrinsic reality and worth. "They are instrumental because they, as it were, make themselves available to each other. In religious idiom, nature is the divine (whether in the guise of one or many actual entities) giving itself . . . that other beings might be nourished and flourish. And in this sense, nature in view of what it really is is intrinsically worthy of respect and gratitude."[20]

Lavely's vision of all things giving of themselves to all things fits in very nicely with the vision of contemplation as all things con-templating or indwelling all things in different degrees. The quality of the giving of oneself outwardly in action (poiesis) is based on the depth of the awareness of one's intrinsic reality or penetration of the whole (theoria). The deeper one's insight, the higher the quality of one's action. Lavely concludes his paper with a conjecture that the joining of personalism and panpsychism may be the last best hope of metaphysics. I believe that the concept of integral yogic contemplation expounded here accomplishes that synthesis and carries it further into the practical realm.

The practicality of contemplation for social ethics requires the model persons of personalism to liberate contemplation from its traditional confinement to the monastery. The model persons envisioned here are those by virtue of accomplishment in both the inward, theoria, and expressive, poiesis, dimensions of contemplation. The integral vision is one not of merely intellectual understanding mechanically applied (the model of the technocrat, as in the mental-rational psychohistorical structure of consciousness), nor of spiritual insight and charismatic influence (the model of the saint, as in the mythic structure), nor of instinctual or elemental enlightenment and empowerment (the model of the shaman, as in the magical structure), but is one that realizes all these temporal structures within an ecological and evolutionary framework of self-unfoldment. In this type of model person people will recognize a relevant ideal for this age and hearken to the call within themselves urging them to realize the potential of their own personhood. Through the example of the integral model person it will become more clear than has been the case that personhood is not confined to the human and God in the traditional monotheistic sense, and that the realization of one's personhood (self-realization) is dependent on recognizing and respecting the universality of personhood in nature and all its beings. If it is true that we are at an evolutionary junction, then what it takes to realize the fullest available measure of personhood today is more than what it took yesterday.

The mechanism of this realization is contemplation. The quality of our actions is based in our contemplation. The environmental crisis is a result and symptom of the deficient quality of our action. The deepening of our contemplative insight into the higher values of nature will raise the quality of our action from the merely utilitarian. The values needed to be realized are not merely traditional values neglected by modernity—an attempted return to which would probably be unsuccessful and, in any case, helpless to counteract the anti-ecological forces of modernity—but emerging values capable of integrating the values actualized by both modernity and antiquity and integrating both the more static, conserving equilibrium of ecological sensitivity with the dynamism of equilibrium-disrupting evolving consciousness.[21]

CONCLUSION

Throughout this discussion various aspects of an integral ecological ethic have been brought to light. Does this sketch provide us with a better alternative than existing environmental ethics? This question, it should be noted, comes loaded with presuppositions which do not fit the case very well. First, the question comes from the mental-rational perspective with an implicit utilitarian standard: which ethic will most likely change our environmentally destructive practices? The quickest change will likely come as a result of legislative action, and legislation operates largely on utilitarian-management ethic principles. Or it may come through judicial action, in which case the rights approach is most appropriate. The answer really depends on how the question is framed. The question defines the problem. Certainly if the environmental crisis is conceived as it has been in this exposition, as a crisis of contemplation, then the answer is clearly the integral ecological ethic outlined here or something like it. However, this way of viewing the crisis is not meant as an alternative to other forms of ethics, in the same way as the deontological approach, for example, is an alternative to the utilitarian. Even if an ideology of integralism should somehow sweep over the world's civilizations today, it would not render all existing forms of environmental ethics as anachronistic. Primarily it is the context in which these ethics operate which will change, and that, of course, will affect the way these ethics are conceived and practiced. Utilitarian and deontological approaches will still be useful, but informed by an integral consciousness they will not as likely be used for ego-/anthropo-centric ends. Deep Ecology would be broadened by integralism without having to sacrifice its basic principle of intuitive identity with nature, thereby lessening its agonistic relationship with nonmagically oriented viewpoints. What integral contemplation accomplishes is the overcoming of the exclusivism of each of the structures of consciousness, which is to say their limited (and hence not fully ecological) contemplation and, at the same stroke, their limited effectiveness in the world of relationship and action. Exclusivism, generally speaking, is the chief defect of the attitudes towards nature criticized in this work. Hence the solution of the ecological crisis will require an end to the exclusivism of the mental-rational structure in education especially. Concerted effort must be made to cultivate the efficient expressions of the heretofore repressed structures, coupled with critique and corrections of the deficient expressions of the structures (for example, the deficient and exploitative use of mythic imagery in the media). This, of course, is no quick fix scheme. In spite of the urgency of the crisis any quick fix is at best only a temporary stay of execution, and because it will be regressive (in direct proportion to its quickness) in character (however revolutionary in ideology) may very well constitute a hindrance to the actualization of the prerequisite for ecological balance, which is the integralization of consciousness. It is hoped, however, that this exposition has demonstrated that what may well be our last resort is really a great opportunity for the human race as well as its fellow travellers in the cosmic journey, Earth and all her beings.

The integral ecological ethic, as I have sketched it, is not so much a practical ethic (in the sense of a set of rules indirectly and mechanically applicable to decision making on concrete issues) as an awareness and intelligence that makes the most appropriate decisions directly without first having to think about which rules or principles to apply. Rational thought, including particular styles of thinking, such as utilitarianism, may be brought to bear upon a situation if the situation requires it. A philosophical ethic is only as good as the intelligence employing it. Consequently, any contemporary philosophical construction of an ethic which neglects the improvement of consciousness or intelligence is not going to provide the basis for a truly ecological lifestyle.

The main thrust of those working from within an integral consciousness should be directed towards the education of moral sensitivity and the extension of contemplative insight. At this emergent stage of the integral structure of consciousness the front line of the educative effort needs be of the educators themselves. Without developing an integral awareness in themselves, educators cannot expect to serve the emergence of the integral persons the next generation needs to counteract the environmental quagmire our generation is bequeathing them.

NOTES

CHAPTER 1

1. This ecological point of view contradicts the apparent thrust of Christianity when the latter takes a supernatural standpoint which sanctions the exploitation of nature for the attainment of a supernatural end. This supernatural end, furthermore, is largely conceived in terms of individual salvation and is thus not contingent on or even responsible for the welfare of future generations. Even so, a growing number of Christian thinkers are offended by the degree of violence against nature which, they argue, far exceeds the limits to exploitation that the God-given responsibility of stewardship imposes upon us. Among the most prominent of these ecologically sensitive theologians are Thomas Berry, John Cobb, Matthew Fox, and Charles Hartshorne. Thomas Berry, arguably the most ecologically conscious theologian today (he styles himself as a geologian), says it is high time that Christianity countered its overemphasis on redemption by cultivating a spiritual appreciation of creation. Perhaps we can expect to see Christians beginning to reexamine the "nature" of the supernatural. Saint Augustine, after all, in the last chapter of *The City of God*, presents us with some very natural chracteristics of the supernatural.

For an historical overview of Christianity's attitudes towards nature see H. Paul Santmire, *The Travail of Nature: The Ambiguous Ecological Promise of Christian Theology* (Philadelphia: Fortress Press, 1985). Santmire traces the developments of two tendencies in Christian theology: the one emphasizing the journey of ascent (away from nature to transcendental redemption); the other emphasizing what Santmire calls the metaphor of fecundity and the metaphor of migration to a good land, these constituting the neglected ecological promise of Christianity.

2. Paul Shepard, a leading ecologically oriented thinker, writes:

Ecological thinking (as opposed to atomistic thinking) requires a kind of vision across boundaries. The epidermis of the skin is ecologically like a pond surface or a forest soil, not a shell so much as a delicate interpenetration. It reveals the self enobled and extended rather than threatened as part of the landscape and ecosystem, because the beauty and complexity of nature are continuous with ourselves.

... It further implies exploration and openness across an inner boundary—an ego boundary—and appreciative understanding of the animal in ourselves which our heritage of Platonism, Christian morbidity, duality, and mechanism have long held repellant and degrading.

... To to so means nothing less than a shift in our whole frame of reference and our attitude toward life itself, a wider perception of the landscape as a creative, harmonious being where relationships of things are as real as the things.

... The pond is an example. Its ecology includes all events: the conversion of sunlight to food and the food-chains within and around it, man drinking, bathing, fishing, plowing the slopes of the watershed, drawing a picture of it, and formulating theories about the world based on what he sees in the pond. He and all the other organisms at and in the pond act upon one another, engage the earth and atmosphere and are linked to other ponds by a network of connections like the threads of protoplasms connecting cells in living tissues. The elegance of such systems and delicacy of equilibrium are the outcome of a long evolution of interdependence. Even society, mind and culture are parts of that evolution.

... Although ecology may be treated as a science, its greater and overriding wisdom is universal. That wisdom can be approached mathematically, chemically, or it can be danced or told as a myth.

... There is only one ecology, not a human ecology on one hand and another for the subhuman. No one school or theory or project or agency controls it.

... The ideological status of ecology is that of a resistance movement. Its Rachel Carsons and Aldo Leopolds are subversive (as Sears recently called ecology itself). They challenge the public or private right to pollute the environment, to systematically destroy preda-tory animals, to spread chemical pesticides indiscriminately, to meddle chemically with food and water, to appropriate without hindrance space and surface for technological and military ends; they oppose the uninhibited growth of human populations, some forms of "aid" to "underdeveloped" peoples, the needless addition of radio-activity to the landscape, the extinction of species of plants and animals, the domestication of all wild places, large-scale manipula-tion of the atmosphere or the sea, and most other purely engineering solutions to problems of and intrusions into the organic world. If naturalists seem always to be *against* something it is because they feel a responsibility to share their understanding, and their opposition constitutes a defense of the natural systems to which man is committed as an organic being.

(*The Subversive Science*, ed. by Paul Shepard and Daniel McKinley [Boston: Houghton Mifflin, 1969], pp 1-10.)

3. The work of Ilya Prigogine sheds much light on this dynamic interdependent and interchanging aspect of living forms. To a much greater extent than non-living systems, living forms are far-from-equilibrium systems. He calls them "dissipative structures" because of their need to constantly dissipate entropy or die into equilibrium. (This presents a more dynamic picture of nature than the "steady-state" theory held by some earlier ecologists.) Dissipative structures survive only by remaining open to a continuous exchange of energy and matter with their environment. Paradoxically, the stability of these structures rests on an instability or total dependence on their environment. This dependence, however, works both ways: nature is not stacked up hierarchically such that the more complex structures depend on the lower and not vice versa. Rather, the introduction of complexity arising from the disequilibrium of less complex structures changes the whole Gestalt of the ecology into one in which all levels are interdependent. Emergent structures and orders of interdependence are real, which is to say that for dissipative structures, being is becoming. Time is irreversible, Prigogine maintains against the Einsteinian notion of spatialized time, or reversibility of time. In fact, "irreversibility is a source of order at all levels. Irreversibility is the mechanism that brings order out of chaos." Time is the creative dynamism of dissipative structures. Or, dissipative structures *are* time.

Time, of course, is inseparable from subjectivity, which is why physicists have so vigorously tried to prove that it is an illusion. In this respect they were mistaken, says Prigogine. Neither reality nor our knowledge of it can be purely objective, for time constitutes both the observer and the observed and binds them together. We live in a participatory universe. It is the stance of the objective, detached observer which is the illusion.
(Ilya Prigogine and Isabelle Stengers, *Order Out of Chaos: Man's New Dialogue with Nature*, [N.Y.: Bantam Books, 1984], especially pages 219-313. For a short overview of Prigogine's work see *Looking Glass Universe: The Emerging Science of Wholeness*, by John Briggs and F. David Peat, [N.Y.: Cornerstone Library, 1984], pages 154-178.)

4. "We can no longer accept the old a priori distinction between scientific and ethical values. This was possible at a time when the external world and our internal world appeared to conflict, to be nearly orthogonal. Today we know that time is a construction and therefore carries an ethical responsibility." (Prigogine, op. cit. p. 312)

5. The relation between nature and ethics depends, of course, on one's picture of nature. Stephen Toulmin cites the two Huxleys, Julian and his grandfather, Thomas Henry, as examples of completely contrary conclusions concerning the ethical import of evolution. Julian sees in evolution definite guidance for ethics which is the outcome of the evolutionary nisus on the human level. T. H., on the other hand, held that "The ethical progress of society depends not on imitating the cosmic process ... but on combatting it." Toulmin concludes that we cannot choose between these views on scientific grounds. (*The Return to Cosmology*, pages 53-71). The position I take in this essay is that although the realm of human thought and values appears to occupy a niche separate from the *natural* realm, these two realms are more closely related than apart by virtue of being subsumed in the total ecology of the earth-cosmos. This is a metaphysical position first and only secondarily seeks confirmation in science.

6. The appelation of psychohistory to Gebser's work is made by Georg Feuerstein in his book *The Essence of Yoga*, (N.Y.: Grove Press, 1974), which is an application of Gebser's method to the study of yoga. He may have gotten the concept from Arnold Toynbee whom he credits as having prepared the ground for this new discipline. "The crux of the psychohistorical approach," writes Feuerstein, "lies in its insight that the contexts and constellations of socio-cultural structures express a definite and definable type of consciousness, and that all transformations in the consciousness substratum are bodied forth in stylistic changes in the diverse domains of cultural life, such as social relationships, art and philosophy, etc. History is understood as a consciousness process. It is, above all, the work of the Swiss cultural philosopher Jean Gebser which has helped to inaugurate this new discipline, although he himself did not use the term 'Psychohistory'." (p. 18) Gebser would not have liked the term insofar as it is "mental-rational," a characterization which we explain below.

Jean Gebser (1905-1971) wrote his magnum opus on psychohistory during World War II. Volume 1 of *Ursprung und Gegenwart*, was published in 1949 and volume 2 in 1953 by Deutsche Verlags-Anstalt GmbH, Stuttgart. The English translation by Noel Barstad and Algis Mickunas, *The Ever-Present Origin*, was published by Ohio University Press in 1984.

7. This argument was made recently by Gerald Larson, quoted here as representative of this view. "Philosophy (including comparative philosophy) as conventionally construed in the modern world since Descartes cannot adequately deal with the environmental crisis. Rather it is a part of the crisis and cannot itself be used as a way of dealing with the crisis. So with all other specializations which are the result of the Weberian process of 'rationalization' which has turned out to be a Freudian defense-mechanism of a highly neurotic world system. Environmental ethics is symptomatic of the crisis." "Conceptual Resources in South Asia for 'Environmental Ethics' or The Fly is

Still Alive and Well in the Bottle." *Philosophy East and West* vol. 37, no. 2 April 1987, p. 154.

8. For an overview of other ancient and modern forms of psycho-historical schemata, see "A Brief Historical Outline of Psychohistories" in *Ecology, Time and Contemplation: An East-West Approach to Environmental Ethics*, by Daniel Kealey (doctoral dissertation, State University of New York at Stony Brook, 1987; available through University Microfilms, 300 N. Zeeb Road, Ann Arbor, MI 48106).

9. "A true process always occurs in quanta, that is, in leaps; or, expressed in quasi-biological and not physical terms, in mutations. It occurs spontaneously, indeterminately, and, consequently, discontinuously. "... the mutational process we are speaking of is spiritual and not biological or historical. [Whereas] "biological mutation leads to a specialization of functions within a particular environment—a minus mutation—consciousness mutation, by contrast, unfolds toward overdetermination: toward structural enrichment and dimensional increment; it is intensifying and inductive—a plus mutation." (Gebser, *The Ever-Present Origin*, [Athens, Ohio: Ohio University Press, 1984] pp 37-8; hereafter referred to as *Origin* in the notes.

10. Ibid., p. 39.

11. Ibid., p. 43.

12. Ibid., p. 44.

13. Ibid., p. 45.

14. Ibid., p. 46.

15. Ibid.

16. Ibid., p. 48.

17. Ibid., p. 162. Perhaps if Gebser had lived to read Carlos Castaneda's *The Teachings of Don Juan* he would have been a little more sanguine about our ability to articulate the magical consciousness. On the other hand, he may then have pointed out that the theoretical, structuralist explanation of magic that Castaneda attempts in the latter part of the book was widely perceived to be not as satisfactory as the descriptive narration in the first part. Castaneda himself abandons all attempts at theorizing in subsequent books and takes on a mythic voice. This is the difference between having the mental speak for the magical and letting the magical speak for itself, which I think is what Gebser is refering to.

One is reminded also of the oft reported accounts of skeptical mystics who lose their vision when trying to touch it to see if it is 'real'. The mental-rational, however, can be trained to observe the prerational in an unbiased way. Such is the purport of phenomenology, for example.

18. Ibid., pp. 162-5.

19. Ibid., p. 67.

20. Ibid., p. 221. Life and death as polar aspects of (psychic) experience is an inconceivable fact for mentalized consciousness, as expressed by Wittgenstein: "Death is not an event in life: we do not live to experience death." (*Tractatus Logico-Philosophicus*, 6.4311) Compare with Chuang Tzu: "The man of virtue . . . can see where all is dark. He can hear where all is still." Or, "Whoever believes Nothingness to be the head, Life to be the backbone, Death to be the tail; Whoever can know life, death, being, and nonbeing all as one, shall be our friend." (*Chuang Tsu*, translation by Gia-fu Feng and Jane English, [N.Y.: Vintage Books, 1974], page 128.)

21. Gebser reports that "the corresponding verb for *mythos* is *mytheomai*, meaning "to discourse, talk, speak"; its root, *mu*, means "to sound". But another verb of the same root, *myein*—ambivalent because of the substitution of the short "u"—means "to close", specifically to close the eyes, the mouth and wounds. From this root we have Sanskrit *mukas* (with long vowel), which means "mute, silent," and Latin *mutus* with the same meaning. It recurs in Greek in the word *mystes*, "the consecrated," and *mysterion*, "mysterium", and later during the Christian era, gave the characteristic stamp to the concept of mysticism: speechless contemplation with closed eyes, i.e., eyes turned inward." (*Origin*, p. 65)

22. I am using the words ambivalence and ambiguity more or less equivalently. Merleau-Ponty in "The Child's Relation with Others" distinguishes these two terms by making ambivalence to refer to psychological rigidity or reaction-formation. Psychological "ambivalence consists of having two alternative images of the same object, the same person, without making any effort to connect them or to notice that in reality they relate to the same object and the same person." (*The Primacy of Perception*, p. 103.) Ambiguity, on the other hand, is nonpathological because it consists in being able to admit to the existence of contradictory traits in the same object or person. Mythic experience would then have to be characterized as ambiguous in the Merleau-Ponty sense, whereas ambivalency would be a deficient mode of mythic experience overdetermined by mental dualism (if it can still be called mythic experience at all, for according to Gebser, ambivalency in the sense employed by Merleau-Ponty is a characteristic of the mental structure). This raises the interesting question whether the mental structure as a whole is a pathological reaction-formation!

23. "Animal" in Greek meant not just subhuman beast, but any animated being, and included gods, demons, the ensouled stars, the anima mundi or World Soul, and even the cosmos as a whole, as well as humans. (see

Hans Jonas, *The Phenomenon of Life: Toward a Philosophical Biology*, [N.Y.: Harper & Row, 1966] p. 227).

24. See James Hillman, *Revisioning Psychology* (N.Y.: Harper & Row, 1975) for an illuminating account of the polytheistic imagination and its work of soul-making.

25. *Origin*, p. 165.

26. Ibid., p. 77.

27. Ibid., pp. 11-23.

28. See *Sacred Discontent: The Bible and Western Tradition*, by Herbert Schneidau (Berkeley: University of California Press, 1977) for whom the prophets are paragons of alienated man.

29. Op. cit., p. 180.

30. "To the perception of the aperspectival world [i.e., integral structure] time appears to be the very fundamental function, and to be of a most complex nature. It manifests itself in accordance with a given consciousness structure and the appropriate possibility of manifestation in its various aspects as clock time, natural time, cosmic or sidereal time; as biological duration, rhythm, meter; as mutation, discontinuity, relativity; as vital dynamics, psychic energy (and thus in a certain sense in the form we call 'soul' and the 'unconscious'), and as mental dividing. It manifests itself as the unity of past, present, and future; as the creative principle, the power of imagination, as work, and even as 'motoricity.' And along with the vital, psychic, biological, cosmic, rational, creative, sociological, and technical aspects of time, we must include—last but not least—physical-geometric time which is designated as the 'fourth dimension'." *Origin*, p. 285.

31. Ibid., p. 99.

32. Ibid.

33. Ibid., p. 287.

34. Ibid., p. 288.
Jeremy Rifkin notes how modern efficiency-worshipping civilization has continuously distanced itself from the biological rhythms of the planet. For the natural rhythms of the sun's daily path and the processions of the seasons we have substituted an artificial time environment monitored by mechanical and electronic devices. The strain that our demand for speeded up efficiency has put on the environment has been evident for some time. But the strain that speeded up time has on the human being is equally depleting, as is becoming more apparent now in the computer age. Computers are now

operating in terms of nanoseconds (a billionth of a second). This introduces a revolution in the way humans relate to time. For the first time, time is organized at a speed that is below the field of consciousness. As we go deeper into increased computerization complex decisions will be made in a time frame that we will never be able to experience. Psychologists have been reporting increased incidences of computer related distress. Many of these problems have to do with the dissonance between adaptation to computer time and switching back to social time. Computer operators are having increased problems with patience and relating to the mores of more natural time frames. (Jeremy Rifkin, "Time wars: A new dimension shaping our future," *Utne Reader* no. 23 Sept./Oct. 1987, p. 46, or his book, *Time Wars: The Primary Conflict in Human History* [N.Y.: Henry Holt & Co., 1987]).

35. Ibid.

36. Ibid., p. 289.
After having exposed the pathologies of speeded up time in contemporary society, Jeremy Rifkin continues,

> Already a number of new movements and constituencies are emerging, each incorporating elements of a radical new attitude toward time. Movements concerned with environmental issues, holistic health, alternative agriculture, animal rights, appropriate technology, Judeo-Christian stewardship, eco-feminism, bioregionalism, economic democracy, alternative education, disarmament, and self-sufficiency are all groping toward a new vision of time.
>
> While the new time rebels acknowledge that increased efficiency has resulted in short-term material benefits, they argue that the long-term psychic and environmental damage has outstripped whatever temporary gains might have been made by the obsession with speed at all costs. They argue that the pace of production and consumption should not exceed nature's ability to recycle wastes and renew basic resources. They argue that the tempo of social and economic life should be compatible with nature's time frame. In the years to come, these new heretics may become a political force to reckon with, as time becomes a central political battleground around the nation and the world. (Op. cit., p. 56-7.)

37. *Origin*, p. 292.

CHAPTER 2

1. This and the following information on Gifford Pinchot is based on the account given by Stephen Fox, *John Muir and His Legacy: The American Conservation Movement* (Boston, 1981) pp. 110-130.

2. Garrett Hardin, *Exploring New Ethics for Survival, the Voyage of the Spaceship Beagle*, (N.Y.: Viking Press, 1972); idem and John Baden, eds, *Managing the Commons*, (San Francisco, 1977).

3. John Passmore, "Attitudes Toward Nature," *Nature and Conduct*, ed. by R.S. Peters (N.Y., 1975).

4. Jeremy Bentham, *The Principles of Morals and Legislation* (1789), chapter XVII, sec. 1. This work is found reprinted in many anthologies of moral philosophy.

5. Peter Singer, *Practical Ethics*, (Cambridge University Press, 1979) p. 92.

6. Tom Regan, "The Case for Animal Rights," *In Defense of Animals*, Peter Singer, ed., (London, 1985), pp. 16-18.

7. Ibid., p. 19.

8. Ibid., p. 23.

9. Ibid., p. 13.

10. Christopher Stone's article was republished in book form: *Should Trees have Standing? Toward Legal Rights for Natural Objects* (Los Altos, Cal.: W. Kaufmann, 1974).
Roderick Nash, "Rounding Out the American Revolution: Ethical Extension and the New Environmentalism," in *Deep Ecology*, Michael Tobias, ed. (San Diego: Avant Books, 1985).

11. Ibid., p. 178.

12. Some of the deep ecology philosophy can be found in the following: Bill Devall & George Sessions, *Deep Ecology*, (Layton, Utah: Peregrine Smith, 1986); idem, "Ecophilosophy," (Sierra College, Rocklin, CA), an annual newsletter whose last year of publication was 1985; Michael Tobias, ed., *Deep Ecology*, (San Diego: Avant Books, 1985); Dolores LaChapelle, *Earth Wisdom*, (Siverton, CO: Finn Hill Arts, 1982), and *Sacred Land Sacred Sex—Rapture of the Deep*, (Silverton, CO: Finn Hill Arts, 1988). Articles on deep ecology and critical discussion of their principles are frequently found in the journal, *Environmental Ethics*.

13. John Rodman, "The Liberation of Nature?" *Inquiry* 20 (Oslo, 1977).

14. Gifford Pinchot, *Breaking New Ground*, (N.Y., 1947), p. 261, quoted in Devall & Sessions, "The Development of Natural Resources and the Integrity of Nature: Contrasting Views of Management," *Environmental Ethics*, (Winter, 1984).

15. Cf., Daniel Dombrowski, *The Philosophy of Vegetarianism*, (Amherst: The University of Massachussetts, 1984).

16. Cf., Peter Singer, *Animal Liberation*, pp. 197-209.

17. "Against the Inevitability of Human Chauvinism," in *Ethics and the Problems of the Twentyfirst Century*, K.E. Goodpaster & K.M. Sayre, eds. (University of Notre Dame, 1979).

18. Richard Rubinstein's *The Cunning of History: The Holocaust & the American Future*, (N.Y.: Harper, 1978), is a meditation on the sociocultural causes of the Holocaust. While it is the vicious turn of the "culture of modernity" which is immediately at fault, he finds the roots go much further back. The Holocaust was not just a case of anti-semitism, but was part of a larger twentieth century phenomenon, the extermination of large numbers of people as a matter of expediency. While most of these people were disenfranchized minorities, the phenomenon was not limited to them, for World War I evinced the willingness of governments to sacrifice millions of their own sons in battles of no consequence. People had become expendable. Extermination had become the most rational and least costly solution of the problem of disposing of a surplus population.

The progress in death-dealing capacity was not only in terms of technological advances in weaponry but also in social organization or bureaucracy. The specific nature of bureaucracy, notes Max Weber, "develops the more perfectly the more bureaucracy is 'dehumanized', the more completely it succeeds in eliminating from official business love, hatred, and all the purely personal, irrational and emotional elements which escape calculation."

Western bureaucracy is founded on fundamental tendencies of the Judeo-Christian religion which have encouraged the processes of secularization, disenchantment of the world, and rationalization. From this it follows that the call for a return to the values of Judeo-Christian culture could hardly be the guarantee against future Holocausts (nuclear or environmental), for it is part of the problem. The *ethos* of the Judeo-Christian West (as opposed to its manifest values) found expression in America in the slavery and exploitation of Africans: no Western (and Westernized developing) country is innocent of this ethos.

One of the ironies of this ethos is the extent to which people will inflict its logical consequences on themselves to their own detriment, tragically demonstrated by the Jewish cooperation in their own extermination. Rubenstein sees no escape from our self-defeating ethos of exclusivism and intolerance rooted in our religious tradition which insists upon the dichotomous division of mankind into the elect and the reprobate. Only a world-wide catastrophe that destroys civilization will bring it to a close, a cure infinitely worse than the disease itself. Perhaps, however, we can learn something from this dilemma and avoid the extremes.

See also, Morris Berman, *The Reenchantment of the World*, (Cornell University, 1981); Fritjof Capra, *The Turning Point*, (N.Y.: Bantam, 1983).

19. He goes on to say, "The better parts of humanism are not in question here; when the inappropriate religious elements have been removed, humanism will become what it ought to be, a gentle and decent philosophy and a trustworthy guide to nondestructive human behavior." David Ehrenfeld, *The Arrogance of Humanism*, (Oxford University Press, 1981), p. 4.

20. Ibid., p. 16-17.

21. Ibid., p. 247.

22. Ibid., p. 91.

23. Ibid., p. 127.

24. Ibid., p. 92.

25. "Simple in Means, Rich in Ends: A Conversation with Arne Naess," by Stephen Bodin, *The Ten Directions*, (Los Angeles Zen Center), Summer/Fall 1982, p. 14.

26. "Deep ecology is ultimately grounded in a *sensibility* (i.e., an openness to emotions and impressions) rather than a *rationality* (i.e., an openness to data ["facts"] and logical inference but an [attempted] closedness to empathic understanding)." Warwick Fox, *Ecophilosophy*, VI, 1984, p. 12.

27. See, for example, Paul Shepard, *The Tender Carnivore and the Sacred Game* (N.Y.: Charles Scribner's Sons, 1973) which posits the ideal of a "future primitive."

28. *The Ten Directions* interview. Ernest Callenbach, *Ecotopia* (Berkeley: Banyon Tree Books, 1975).

29. Bill Devall & George Sessions, *Deep Ecology*, p. 67.

30. John Livingston, *One Cosmic Instant: Man's Fleeting Supremacy*, (N.Y.: Houghton Mifflin, 1973), p. 175.

31. Ibid., p. 80.

32. Devall & Sessions, *Deep Ecology*, p. 71.

33. Ibid., p. 67-8.

34. Jim Dodge, "Living by Life: Some Bioregional Theory and Practice," *The Co-Evolution Quarterly*, Winter, 1981. Compare with Heidegger: "Dwelling is not primarily inhabiting but taking care of *(schonen)* and creating that space within which something comes into its own and flourishes. Dwelling is primarily saving *(retten)*, in the older sense of setting something free to become

itself, what it essentially is . . . . Dwelling is that which cares for things so that they essentially presence and come into their own . . . ." (*The Piety of Thinking*, quoted by Delores LaChapelle, *Earth Wisdom*, p. 82).

35. Wendell Berry, in *The Unsettling of America: Culture and Agriculture*, (N.Y.: Avon Books, 1977), writes eloquently of the avaricious and vicious effects of this pioneering spirit on American agriculture and culture. While "the first and greatest American revolution, which has never been superseded, was the coming of people who did *not* look upon the land as a homeland," (p. 4) there have always been those who countered this tendency by deciding to stay and live in a nurturing relationship with the land. They developed the small farm agricultural tradition which is now being destroyed by the combined organizational efforts of agri-business, academic specialists and technicians, and government bureaucrats. The opposing forces are characterized thusly by Berry: "The competence of the exploiter is in organization; that of the nurturer is in order—a human order, that is, that accommodates itself both to other order and to mystery. The exploiter typically serves an institution or organization; the nurturer serves land, household, community, place. The exploiter thinks in terms of numbers, quantities, 'hard facts'; the nurturer in terms of character, condition, quality, kind." (p. 8)

The incompatibility of these two orientations in a nonexpanding country is being witnessed today with the alarming disappearance of the small farmers who are unable to become efficient and exploitive businessmen ("Get big or get out!" is the advice of the Secretary of Agriculture). The danger in this phenomenon is clear: "The cost of this corporate totalitarianism in energy, land, and social disruption will be enormous. It will lead to the exhaustion of farmland and farm culture. Husbandry will become an extractive industry; because maintenance will entirely give way to production, the fertility of the soil will become a limited, unrenewable resource like coal or tar." (p. 10) "A healthy *farm* culture," on the other hand, "can be based only upon familiarity and can grow only among a people soundly established upon the land; it nourishes and safeguards a human intelligence of the earth that no amount of technology can satisfactorily replace."(p. 43)

36. Kirkpatrick Sale, *Dwellers in the Land: The Bioregional Vision*, (San Francisco: Sierra Club Books, 1985), p. 42.

37. For a critique of Deep Ecology from an anarchistic perspective see "How Deep is Deep Ecology?" by George Bradford in *Fifth Estate*, vol. 22, no. 3 (327) Fall 1987, and the commentaries and replies, "Delving Deeper into Deep Ecology," which also analyzes the right-wing tendencies of the deep ecology espousing organization Earth First! in their Spring 1988 issue, vol. 23, no. 1 (328). Obtainable from: The Fifth Estate, Box 02548, Detroit, MI 48202 USA.

CHAPTER 3

1. William Irwin Thompson, *The Time Falling Bodies Take to Light: Mythology, Sexuality & the Origins of Culture* (N.Y.: St. Martin's Press, 1981) p. 247-8.

2. Ibid., p. 5.

3. Ibid., p. 10.

4. Ibid., p. 196.

5. Ibid., p. 210.

6. Ibid., pp. 10-13.

7. Various anthropologists and biologists have observed that what differentiates the human species from animals is not reason or tools but man's unspecialization in regards to his living milieu. Humans are not specialized in that they do not come into the world already prepared and equipped to occupy a certain predefined niche. Man is in a perpetual embryonic state, hence always evolving. To become specialized, as in the developing of claws or prehensile tails, is to reach the end of an evolutionary trajectory: there is no longer an openness to developing other possibilities. Biologist Norman Macbeth recounts a line of biological speculation called fetalization. A baby chimpanzee, he tells us, looks like a little old man, but as it grows it loses the human look. Man is closely related to the chimpanzee but has managed to vastly prolong the fetal stage of the chimpanzee, growing larger but not developing the large jaws and other nonhuman traits that the chimpanzee descends into. According to this line of reasoning, Thompson's making the mythic structure a specialization of consciousness effectively closes humanity off from an open evolutionary future. See Norman Macbeth, *Darwinism: A Time for Funerals* (Mill Valley, Cal.: Robert Briggs Associates, 1985), p. 14-15.

8. In his Introduction to *Revelation* by David Spangler, Thompson writes about the new age in terms that are more integral than mythic:

> Planetary man will not learn how to humanize technology by thinking like a machine, he will humanize technology through animism. *The new culture is the consummation of all previous cultures, for only the combined energy of our entire cultural history is equal to the new landscape of Findhorn . . . . And so there will be scientists and mystics in the New Age.* (my emphasis).

9. See *Findhorn—A Center of Light* by Paul Hawken (Boston: East-West Journal/Tao Publications, 1974). The message of Findhorn finds its most philosophical voice in David Spangler's *Revelation: The Birth of a New Age* (San Francisco: The Rainbow Bridge, 1976). The mythic phenomenon is found also

in places not related to Findhorn. See, for example, *Behaving As If The God In All Life Mattered: A New Age Ecology* by Machaelle Small Wright (Perelandra, Jeffersonton, VA, 1987), and *Talking With Nature: Sharing the Energies and Spirit of Trees, Plants, Birds, and Earth* by Michael J. Roads (H.J. Kramer: Tiburon, CA, 1987).

10. Skolimowski's major works in this area are, *Eco-Philosophy*, (N.Y.: Marion Boyars, 1981); *Eco-Theology*, (Ann Arbor, MI: Eco-Philosophy Centre, 1985); and *The Theatre of the Mind*, (Wheaton, IL: Quest Books, 1984).

11. "Present analytic philosophy is an embodiment of the positivist ethos, which is based on the cult of technique and the avoidance of problems. Analytic philosophy is not a liberation of the mind (as its practitioners want to insist), but a confinement of the mind in the circus of technical virtuosity. The endless debates over, for example, 'sense' and 'reference' by the 'leading philosophers' of the 'outstanding intellectual centres', such as Oxford and Cambridge, Harvard and Princeton, Berkeley and Ann Arbor, is a curious spectacle. The same positions, arguments and resolutions have been repeated over and over again during the past fifty years! With Frege and Russell, Lesniewski and Tarski, the creative aspects of the problem have been explored and exhausted. The last forty years of the debate therefore represents tedious scholasticism resolving itself in pedantic linguistic exercises. The trivialization of problems and of minds is the price we pay for spurious technical virtuosity." (*Eco-Philosophy*, p. 20.)

12. Ibid., p. 23.

13. See George Session's book review of Skolimowski's *Eco-Philosophy*, in *Environmental Ethics*, vol. 6, Summer 1984, pp. 167-174.

14. "The New Story" is what "geologian" Thomas Berry calls the new understanding of cosmic evolution, largely inspired by Teilhard de Chardin, but carried on with the speculative vision emerging from the New Physics and evolutionary biology, as well as ecology. See his "The New Story" first published in *Teilhard Studies*, and reprinted in the *Riverdale Papers on the Earth Community* (Riverdale Center of Religious Research, Riverdale, N.Y., n.d.). The New Story is told at length in dialogue form by Brian Swimme, *The Universe is a Green Dragon: A Cosmic Creation Story* (Santa Fe, N.M.: Bear & Co., 1985).

15. *Eco-Philosophy*, p. 54-5.

16. Pierre Teilhard de Chardin is best known for *The Phenomenon of Man* (N.Y.: Harper & Row, 1959); John Cobb's major statement on ecology and religion is *Is It Too Late? A Theology of Ecology* (Beverly Hills, Cal.: Bruce Books, 1972) and *The Liberation of Life*, co-authored with biologist Charles Birch (Cambridge University Press, 1981).

17. Skolimowski, "The Dogma of Anti-Anthropocentrism and Eco-philosophy," *Environmental Ethics*, vol. 6, Fall 1984, p. 284.

18. Ibid., p. 287.

19. *The Theatre of the Mind*, ch. 3.

20. See *Darwinism: A Time for Funerals*, by Norman Macbeth. A summary critique of Darwinism is found in Jeremy Rifkin, *Algeny: A New Word—A New World* (Baltimore: Penguin Books, 1984).

21. *The Theatre of the Mind*, p. 32.

22. *Eco-Philosophy*, p. 76.

23. Ibid., p. 77.

24. Ibid., p. 78.

25. Visceral or emotional metaphors are here not entirely metaphoric, for as Gebser has made clear, an expression of the magical structure, such as deep ecology, finds its primary agency of energy in instinct and emotion. I think this is readily seen in Livingston's opposition to anthropocentrism: "Anyone who has spent the greater part of a lifetime enjoying and attempting to understand and preserve wild nature will have had the experience of witnessing his own species drift lower and lower on his personal scale of perfection. All the magnificence and nobility of our creativity cannot begin to compensate one for toxic pesticides, Bach cannot compensate me for Hiroshima, nor Michelangelo for the blue whale. Jesus Christ can not compensate me for the brutal [sic] imposition of human power over nonhuman nature. Yet, the total destruction of blue Earth may well precede any diminishment in human pride." (John Livingston, *One Cosmic Instant*, p. 188).

The negative *feeling* towards humanity expressed by some Deep Ecologists, however, suggests a deficient form of the prerational feeling orientation of consciousness. The Deep Ecology-oriented *Earth First!* newsletter, for example, has a regular editorial column penned by "Miss Ann Thropy."

26. The *parinamavada* of Sankhya and the Tantric tradition outlines an evolution of consciousness preceded by an involution of the divine. While the Sankhyan worldview was definitely circular, in that the outcome of this entire labor of involution and evolution was identical to the starting point, in the Tantric tradition there are some expressions of the open-endedness of evolution in which the outcome of unity-in-diversity is an evolutionary advance over primal unity. Georg Feuerstein, who employed Gebser's hermeneutic of psychohistory to his analysis of yogic doctrines, classified Tantra as an expression of the holistic-integral structure of consciousness, as

opposed to other schools of yoga which belong properly to the magic-mythic structures. (See *The Essence of Yoga: A Contribution to the Psychohistory of Indian Civilization*). If Feuerstein is correct, then those prima facie mythic expressions of evolution are not really mythic but actually early expressions of integral consciousness.

27. Skolimowski, "The Interactive Mind in the Participatory Universe," *World & I*, (Washington, D.C.: Washington Times), vol. 1, no. 2, February 1986, p. 458.

28. Jean E. Charon, "The Roots of Behavior in Contemporary Physics," *World & I*, (Washington, D.C.: Washington Times), vol. 1, no. 2, February 1986, p. 288.

29. Ibid., p. 289.

30. "The Interactive Mind," p. 467.

31. *Theatre of the Mind*, p. 26.

32. "To define the human being as a sensitive animal, as one who forms himself through the acquisition and enlargement of his sensitivities, is to pay homage to the openness of man's future and also pay homage to the attainments of evolution. The right concept of man is one which acknowledges all man's past attainments but which at the same time makes man open to future refinements, to the acquisitions of the power of consciousness far beyond anything we have so far attained. It is not only, and not so much capacity for, rational thinking or the capacity for making tools that we shall have to cultivate in order to become more than we are at present; we shall have to evoke new sensitivities, some of which are yet undreamed of, some of which are given to us in rudimentary forms such as telepathy, but all of which signify and delineate our being in the sensitive and self-sensitizing cosmos." (*Theatre of the Mind*, p. 29.)

33. "The Interactive Mind in the Participating Universe," p. 462-3.

34. Ibid., pp. 463-5.

35. The concept of a participatory universe may have been first formulated in scientific circles by astrophysicist John Archibald Wheeler, who said, "The universe does not exist 'out there' independent of us. We are inescapably involved in bringing about that which appears to be happening. We are not only observers. We are participators. In some strange sense this is a *participatory universe*." quoted in *Theatre of Mind*, p. 161.

36. Ibid., c. 19.

37. Samual Alexander, *Space, Time, and Deity* (N.Y.: Humanities Press, 1964).

38. Jan Smuts, *Holism and Evolution* (N.Y.: Macmillan, 1926).

39. Ervin Laszlo, *Introduction to Systems Philosophy* (N.Y.: Gordon & Breach, 1972).

40. Skolimowski, *Eco-Theology*, p. 35. Georg Feuerstein informs me that Gebser has expressed the opinion that hope is a disease.

41. *Eco-Philosophy*, p. 35.

CHAPTER 4

1. Cf. Seyyed Hossein Nasr, *The Encounter of Man and Nature*, (London, 1968), p. 14.

2. Rosemary Radford Ruether, *Liberation Theology: Human Hope Confronts Christian History and American Power* (N.Y.: Paulist Press, 1972), p. 115.

3. *Ennead* III.8.1, A.H. Armstrong, trans., (Harvard University Press, Loeb Classical Library, 1980). Subsequent references to this translation will be placed in parentheses after the citation.

4. According to Peter Manchester this statement is actually an interpretive simplification of what Parmenides wrote. "The self-identity expressed [in the line of Parmenides' text, 'Now these are the same: thinking, and that on account of which there is the thought upon.'] is a purely formal statement of the structure of intentional analysis *(noesis-noema)*. It is in no way extensional; it involves no hopeless confusion between 'logic' and 'reality', as *does* the notorious school-Platonic misquote, which is certainly not authentic: 'For the same are Mind and Being.'" ("Parmenides and the Need for Eternity," *Monist*, January 1979, vol. 62, no. 1, p. 97). I would not accuse Plotinus, however, of a "hopeless confusion between 'logic' and 'reality': in the innermost recess of consciousness the boundary between self and not-self is transcended.

5. Cf. Plato's *Symposium* 210.

6. See John Deck, *Nature, Contemplation, and the One*, (Toronto, 1967), p. 20.

7. R.T. Wallis, *Neoplatonism*, (London: Duckworth, 1972), p. 65.

8. This contemplative understanding of action is virtually identical to the concept of *nishkama karma*, desireless action, of the *Bhagavad Gita*, and, mutatis mutandis, to the *wu-wei*, nonaction, of Taoism.

9. In a note to his translation of *Ennead* III.8.7, Armstrong observes that "by making *theoria* the end of all perception and action Plotinus abolishes, no

doubt consciously and deliberately, Aristotle's distinction between *praktike* and *theoretike episteme*, or *dianoia* . . . and makes the whole life, not only of man but the universe, philosophy in Aristotle's sense."

10. The utility of play for the cultivation of nature awareness is demonstrated in the following practical guides: *Sharing the Joy of Nature* by Joseph Cornell (Nevada City, CA: Dawn Publications, 1989); and *Nature, Children, and You* by Paul Goff (Ohio University Press, 1981).

CHAPTER 5

1. Stephen Fox devotes a chapter on the interest many of the leaders of conservation movement had in Asian religions in his book, *John Muir and His Legacy: The American Conservation Movement.*

2. Pantheism has been characterized as Pan-Satanism. Schopenhauer's philosophy was regarded by Otto Liebmann as a sort of Pan-Satanism.
Cf. Hans Jonas, *The Gnostic Religion* (Boston: Beacon Press, 1958), particularly the Epilogue, "Gnosticism, Nihilism, and Existentialism"; and Carl Raschke, *The Interruption of Eternity: Modern Gnosticism and the Origins of the New Religious Consciousness* (Chicago: Nelson-Hall, 1980).

3. Mixing of East and West is still abhorrent to many Western philosophers. The absurd resistance on the part of Western scholars of Neoplatonism to admit any influence of Indian philosophy on Plotinus is indicative of how deeply entrenched this philosophical xenophobia of "Orientalism" is (cf. Edward Said, *Orientalism* (N.Y.: Vintage Books, 1979)). The problem, or symptom, may also indicate the cure. To quote Simone Weil:

> It seems that Europe requires genuine contacts with the East in order to remain spiritually alive. It is also true that there is something in Europe which opposes the Oriental spirit, something specifically Western, . . . and we are in danger of being devoured by it . . . .
> European civilization is a combination of the Oriental spirit with its opposite, and in that combination there needs to be a high proportion of the former. This proportion is today not nearly high enough. We need an injection of the Oriental spirit.

(*Selected Essays*, 1934-43, ed. and trans. Richard Rees (London: Oxford University Press, 1962), p. 205.

4. There are numerous works on Sri Aurobindo. Some of these are: *Sri Aurobindo: Prophet of Life Divine* (San Francisco: Cultural Integration Fellowship, 1973), and *The Integral Philosophy of Sri Aurobindo* (London: George Allen & Unwin, 1960) by Haridas Chaudhuri; *Sri Aurobindo or the Adventure of Conscious-*

ness, by Satprem (Pondicherry, India: Sri Aurobindo Ashram, 1973); *The Essential Aurobindo*, edited by Robert McDermott (N.Y.: Schocken, 1973); "Special Centenary Symposium on the Thought of Sri Aurobindo (1872-1950)" in *The International Philosophical Quarterly*, XII (June 1972).

Sri Aurobindo's philosophical magnum opus is *The Life Divine* (N.Y.: E. P. Dutton, 1951). The other major work from which this essay draws is *The Synthesis of Yoga* (Pondicherry, India: Sri Aurobindo Ashram, 1971); "All life is Yoga" is the epigraph of this book.

Born Aurobindo Ghose, he is known as Sri Aurobindo.

5. *The Synthesis of Yoga*, p. 2.

6. Ibid. The "Great Mother" indicates Aurobindo's personalistic orientation, although he does not insist on it (i.e., the same cn be characterized impersonally, but not as adequately in his view). The Mother or Goddess is the manifest, dynamic aspect of Brahman, not inferior to "Him" because not different essentially. This is a principle that lies at the core of the Tantric tradition.

7. Ibid., p. 3.

8. Sri Aurobindo, *Dictionary of Sri Aurobindo's Yoga* (Pondicherry, India: Sri Aurobindo Ashram, 1973), p. 310.

9. Aurobindo wants to maintain Brahman's absolute transcendence on the one hand while on the other wants that the knowledge by identity with the absolute transcendental infinity be within the grasp of immanent, finite consciousness. His attempt to do so falls within the philosophical tradition of *parināmavāda*, which holds that all evolutes are emanations or transformations of Brahman itself. The parinamavada is opposed to the *vivartavāda* which holds that evolutes are incommensurate with Brahman itself and, as such, cannot logically be derived from it. According to the vivartavādins, realization of Brahman's nature entails the cessation of individuality. Being a realist, Aurobindo is keen to argue that the knowledge of Brahman as *saccidānanda* is valid and that the acknowledgement of that which transcends saccidānanda does not invalidate or sublate it. (According to Aurobindo 'sublate' does not mean to overcome or destroy and preserve another, but is a process of self-transformation, as when Being becomes Non-Being and vice versa; v., *Glossary of Terms in Sri Aurobindo's Writings* [Sri Aurobindo Ashram, 1978] p. 300). The upshot of this view is that enlightenment or the realization of one's identity with Brahman does not entail the disappearance of the phenomenal world as maintained by the vivartavādins of the Advaita Vedānta school.

Aurobindo's position is actually entirely conforming to the intent of Advaitic thought which attempts to tread the razor's edge between ontologizing and disontologizing. On the one hand it strives to experience Being and Brahman, while on the other it diligently tries to avoid the seduction of representative (Heidegger's 'metaphysical' and 'onto-theological') thinking by means of the sword of negation or disontologizing. Hence transcendental experience has two aspects: *nirguna* (negational transcendence) and *saguna* (affirmation of divinity). Because of the stress given to the former, it is a mistake to think of Advaitic speculation as of the same order as Western theology. For Advaita, philosophy and Yoga are inseparable.

10. See *The Life Divine*, p. 368-70.

11. A uniquely creative attempt to articulate an environmental ethic based on play can be found in Joseph Meeker, *The Comedy of Survival: In Search of an Environmental Ethic* (Los Angeles: Guild of Tutors Press, 1980). Meeker contrasts two ethical orientations on the basis of the literary styles that express them. The one is literary tragedy and the other is comedy. Tragedy represents par excellence the Western worldview and ethical orientation. The tragic view assumes that humanity is such that it is always in conflict with powers greater than itself. These forces, whether they be gods, the moral law, passion, the compelling greatness of religious and ideological ideas, exercise controlling influence over human affairs. Though man may at times feel overwhelmed by the conflict generated by the pull of these forces, tragic literature and philosophy uphold the faith in man's ability to stand up to his conflict and be superior to it. In taking his conflict seriously, the tragic man is obsessed with the task of affirming his mastery and greatness even in the face of his own destruction brought on by this tragic choice. The tragic choice is necessitated by a worldview which has simplified the complex world into two camps, the good and the bad, and the consequent assumption that resolution can only be effected by the total triumph of the one and the destruction of the other. By virtue of his purified moral nature, tragic man believes himself to transcend natural limitations and that this entitles him to endow his egoic individualism with supreme importance, as the end for which nature exists.

Comedy, on the other hand, demonstrates man's weaknesses and follies rather than his supernatural strength and rationality. But in spite of his humble posture, the comic character survives. He survives because he doesn't fall prey to morality, goodness, truth, beauty, heroism, patriotism and all such abstract values. Whereas these values purport to ennoble, in the final analysis they cause division, strife and perdition, not only for those to whom they are directed against but to those that hold them. "Comedy is a celebration, a ritual renewal of biological welfare as it persists in spite of any reasons there may be for feeling metaphysical despair." (p. 39) "In the world revealed by comedy, the important thing is to live and to encourage life even though it is probably meaningless to do so. But to deny meaning to life does not make survival trivial, and if survival is not trivial, neither is comedy." (p. 41)

Comedy, argues Meeker, reflects the structure of nature better than any other genre. "Productive and stable ecosystems are those which minimize destructive aggression, encourage maximum diversity, and seek to establish equilibrium among their participants—which is essentially what happens in literary comedy." (p. 41) The evolutionary process, being one of adaptation, accommodation and opportunism, is more of a gigantic comic drama, Meeker finds, than the bloody tragic spectacle imagined by the "sentimental humanists of early Darwinism." Readers familiar with Chinese philosophy will notice the interesting parallels between Meeker's comic ethic and Taoism.

Meeker's insightful analysis of the tragic frame of mind in the West from which we need some comic relief is limited by his refusal to step beyond the blinders of Western culture. His view of tragedy and consequently his rejection of it is thoroughly Western. The alternative model that he proposes is entirely founded on ethology, the upshot of which is that if only we would be true to the animal in us we would be more playful, take ourselves less seriously, live and let live. While such a view provides a much needed corrective to the alienation and promethean hubris stemming from our modern worldview, it is philosophically naive. A soul journey across the world could effect a larger—more global, less provincial—understanding of both the grave or noble and the playful, unassuming dimensions of life, such that one is no longer obliged to choose between one side of the duality or the other, for they are now seen as complementary sides of a greater harmony. Such is *līla*.

12. Aurobindo claims to have been able to scrutinize Brahman at least enough to be able to delineate the essential structure or nature of its līla.

"The Absolute Reality is indefinable and ineffable by mental thought and mental language; it is self-existent and self-evident to itself, as all absolutes are self-evident, but our mental affirmatives and negatives, whether taken separatively or together, cannot limit or define it. But at the same time there is a spiritual consciousness, a spiritual knowledge, a knowledge by identity which can seize the Reality in its fundamental aspects and its manifested powers and figures. All that is comes within this description and, if seen by this knowledge in its own truth or its occult meaning, can be regarded as an expression of the Reality and itself a reality." (*The Life Divine*, page 587).

13. Cf. S. K. Maitra, *The Meeting of the East and West in Sri Aurobindo's Philosophy* (Pondicherry, India: Sri Aurobindo Ashram, 1968), pp. 50-58.

14. "The principle of the process of evolution is a foundation, from that foundation an ascent, in that ascent a reversal of consciousness and, from the greater height and wideness gained, an action of change and new integration of the whole nature." (*The Life Divine*, p. 645). See further in the same work, Book II, ch. 18, "The Evolutionary Process—Ascent and Integration."

15. See *The Life Divine* bk. II, ch. 20, "The Philosophy of Rebirth;" and also Aurobindo's *The Problem of Rebirth* (Pondicherry, India: Sri Aurobindo Ashram, 1973). Jean Gebser also believed in reincarnation as a process in which the individual is enabled to mature toward the integral consciousness. He held

that its recognition is a precondition for awakening the sense of "primal trust," the antidote to the "primal fear" which keeps the individual consciousness bound to the narrow egocentric perspective. See Georg Feuerstein, *Structures of Consciousness* (Lower Lake, Cal.: Integral Publishing, 1987), p. 169.

16. See Aurobindo's *The Future Evolution of Man*, ed. by P.B. Saint-Hilaire (Pondicherry, India: Sri Aurobindo Ashram, 1971).

17. Haridas Chaudhuri, *Sri Aurobindo: Prophet of Life Divine*, p. 47.

18. See *The Integral Yoga of Sri Aurobindo* by Rishabhchand (Pondicherry, India: Sri Aurobindo Ashram, 1959), especially pp. 425-440, "The Integral Transformation."

19. This may not have been exactly how Aurobindo expressed his concern, but Integral Yoga's ecological dimension is very apparent in the utopian community founded by his followers, Auroville, where much work is being done in reclaiming ecologically devastated land.

20. Synairesis, according to Gebser, does for the integral consciousness what synthesis does in the mental-rational consciousness. It lifts up in its diaphanous embrace mental systematization, mythic symbolization, magical participation and all other structural modes of apprehending the world, giving birth to its own method of "arational systasis."

21. "If we could be aware of all the present, all the action of physical, vital, mental energies at work in the moment, it is conceivable that we would be able to see their past too involved in them and their latent future or at least to proceed from present to past and future knowledge. And under certain conditions this might create a sense of real and ever-present time continuity, a living in the behind and the front as well as the immediate, and a step farther might carry us into an ever present sense of our existence in infinite time and in our timeless self, and its manifestation in eternal time might then become real to us and also we might feel the timeless Self behind the worlds and the reality of his eternal world manifestation." (Aurobindo, *The Synthesis of Yoga*, p. 858).

CHAPTER 6

1. Egoism, which represents the full embodiment of the dualistic worldview, can produce either a positive (Thou shalt!) or a negative (Thou shalt not!) ethic, neither of which is integral. Some elucidation of this difference between egocentric and ecocentric or integral ethics can be drawn from Zen ethics based on Dogen's philosophy, which differentiates between thinking, not-thinking, and without-thinking. Thinking is the positive,

conceptually structured mode of apprehending the world; not-thinking is the deliberate suppression of the thinking mode undertaken to achieve a nondifferentiated apprehension of the world. Both are modes that are ego-driven, although the latter is often falsely supposed to be trans-ego (and often involves a regression to pre-egoic states). Without-thinking is the true goal of Zen, however, and it neither upholds nor suppresses either thinking or non-thinking. According to Kasulis, only that ethics based in without-thinking can allow "compassion without distinctions and wisdom without presuppositions." (T. P. Kasulis, *Zen Action/Zen Person* [Honolulu: University of Hawaii, 1981], p. 98). Gebser held that the Zen enlightenment was of an integral consciousness: see *Origin*, p. 222, and Feuerstein, *Structures of Consciousness*, p. 172-174.

2. "In love there is no attempting to fix an objective, no deliberate shaping of purpose, aimed at the higher value and its realization; *love itself, in the course of its own movement*, is what brings about the continuous *emergence* of ever-higher value in the object—just as if it was streaming out from the object of its own accord, without any sort of exertion (even of wishing) on the part of the lover. We may take love to consist in the mere fact that a value already present beforehand comes to light at this point . . . . True love opens our spiritual eyes to ever-higher values in the object loved. It enables us to *see* and does not blind them (as suggested in a most foolish proverb, which obviously thinks of love in terms of a mere impulse of sensual passion)." Max Scheler, *The Nature of Sympathy*, Peter Heath, trans. (Hamden, CT: Archon Books, 1970), p. 157.

3. Max Scheler, *Ressentiment*, William Holdheim, trans. (N.Y.: Schocken Books, 1972) p. 149.

4. The case of the Taoist critique of Confucianism is evidence that the problem of adequacy in morality is not only a modern dilemma, but one intimately tied to the mental structure and the development of patriarchal civilization, which Taoism opposed.

5. In a private conversation, Erazim Kohak, author of *The Embers and the Stars: A Philosophical Inquiry into the Moral Sense of Nature* (The University of Chicago Press, 1984), who bases much of his work on Husserl's phenomenology, expressed how irked he was to have his work labeled as "environmental ethics."

6. I have been deeply influenced in this conception of contemplation by my former teacher, the late Professor Haridas Chaudhuri. Cf. his books, *Integral Yoga* (San Francisco: California Institute of Asian Studies, 1965) esp. pp. 37-52, 83-116; *Mastering the Problems of Living* (N.Y.: Citadel Press, 1968), esp. pp. 158-222; and, *The Evolution of Integral Consciousness* (Wheaton, Ill.: Quest Books, 1977), esp. pp. 15-42, 117-130.

7. This, as we have seen, is *ressentiment*. The Italian psychoanalyst

Roberto Assagioli called it "repression of the sublime," which is as real as the repression of the sexual instinct emphasized by Freud: *Psychosynthesis* (N.Y.: Viking Press, 1971).

8. See Michael Polanyi, *Personal Knowledge* (University of Chicago Press, 1958), pp. 54-65, 160-171, 195-202.

9. Michael Polanyi, *The Study of Man* (University of Chicago Press, 1959), p. 95.

10. Ibid., p. 96.

11. Max Scheler, *Formalism in Ethics and Non-Formal Ethics of Values*, Manfred Frings & Roger Funk, trans. (Evanston, Ill.: Northwestern University Press, 1973), p. 573.

12. Scheler, *Formalism in Ethics*, p. 574.

13. Ibid., p. 580.

14. See Alfonse Deeken, *Process and Permanence in Ethics: Max Scheler's Moral Philosophy* (N.Y.: Paulist Press, 1974), p. 216.

15. "The definition of physical nature is, the total of spatial phenomena and their laws. This nature is throughout effect, and contains no causation and no necessity in it." (Borden P. Bowne, *Metaphysics* [Boston University Press, 1943], p. 262).
"To say that this is a universe of purpose means that everything that is is in some sense controlled by purpose, that nothing is real save purposing beings, namely persons. In such a universe there is a Supreme Person and such other persons as his purpose may will to exist; physical nature is real only as the concrete functioning of the purpose of the Supreme Person . . . ." (Edgar Sheffield Brightman, *An Introduction to Philosophy* [N.Y.: Henry Holt, 1951], p. 262).
"The world of space objects which we call nature is no substantial existence by itself, and still less a self-running system apart from intelligence, but only the flowing expression and means of communication of those personal beings. It is throughout dependent, instrumental, and phenomenal." (Bowne, *Personalism* [N.Y.: Houghton Mifflin, 1908], p. 278). Quoted by Frederick Ferre, "Personalism and the Dignity of Nature," *Personalist Forum* vol. 2, no. 1 Spring 1986, p. 9, 11.

16. Brightman, *Person and Reality* (N.Y.: Ronald Press, 1958), p. 202. Quoted by Ferre, ibid., p. 25.

17. Ibid., p. 21.

18. John Lavely, "Personalism Supports the Dignity of Nature," *Personalist Forum* vol. 2, no. 1 Spring 1986, p. 31.

19. Ibid., p. 33.

20. Ibid., p. 34.

21. "The integral knowledge admits the valid truths of all views of existence, valid in their own field, but it seeks to get rid of their limitations and negations and to harmonise and reconcile these partial truths in a larger truth which fulfils all the many sides of our being in the one omnipresent Existence." (Aurobindo, *The Life Divine*, p. 594).

REFERENCES

Augustine, St. *The City of God*. Washington: Catholic University of America Press, 1950-54.

Baden, J., and Hardin, G., eds. *Managing the Commons*. San Francisco: Sierra Club Books, 1977.

Bentham, J. *The Utilitarians: An Introduction to the Principles of Morals and Legislation*. New York: Doubleday, 1961.

Berry, W. *The Unsettling of America*. New York: Avon Books, 1977.

Berry, T. *Riverdale Papers on the Earth Community*. Riverdale, N.Y.: Riverdale Center of Religious Research, n.d.

Bodin, S. "Simple in Means, Rich in Ends: A Conversation with Arne Naess." *The Ten Directions*. Los Angeles: Zen Center, Summer/Fall, 1982.

Bonifazi, C. *The Soul of the World*. Lanham, Md.: University Press of America, 1980.

Briggs, J., and Peat, F. D. *Looking Glass Universe: The Emerging Science of Wholeness*. New York: Cornerstone Library, 1984.

Callenbach, E. *Ecotopia*. Berkeley: Banyon Tree Books, 1975.

Castaneda, C. *The Teachings of Don Juan*. Berkeley: University of California Press, 1971.

Charon, J. "The Roots of Behavior in Contemporary Physics." *World & I*. Washington: Washington Times, February 1966, pp. 287-293.

Chaudhuri, H. *Sri Aurobindo: Prophet of Life Divine*. San Francisco: Cultural Integration Fellowship, 1973.

Chuang Tzu. *Chuang-Tsu: Inner Chapters.* Trans. by English, J., and Feng, Gia-fu. New York: Vintage Books, 1974.

Deck, J. *Nature, Contemplation and the One.* Toronto: University of Toronto Press, 1967.

Deeken, A. *Process and Permanence in Ethics.* New York: Paulist Press, 1974.

Devall, B., and Sessions, G. *Deep Ecology.* Layton, Utah: Peregrine Smith, 1986.

——— "The Development of Natural Resources and the Integrity of Nature: Contrasting Views of Management." *Environmental Ethics* 6:293-322.

Dodge, J. "Living by Life: Some Bioregional Theory and Practice." *Co-Evolution Quarterly* Winter, 1981, pp. 6-12.

Dombrowski, D. *The Philosophy of Vegetarianism.* Amherst: University of Massachussetts Press, 1984.

Ehrenfeld, D. *The Arrogance of Humanism.* London: Oxford University Press, 1981.

Ferre, F. "Personalism and the Dignity of Nature." *Personalist Forum* 2:1-28.

Feuerstein, G. *The Essence of Yoga.* New York: Grove Press, 1974.

——— *Structures of Consciousness: The Genius of Jean Gebser.* Lower Lake, Cal.: Integral Publishing, 1987.

——— *What Color Is Your Consciousness?* Los Angeles: Robert Briggs, 1989.

Fox, S. *John Muir and His Legacy.* Boston: Little, Brown, 1981.

Gebser, J. *The Ever-Present Origin.* Trans. by Barstad, N., and Mickunas, A. Athens, Ohio: Ohio University Press, 1984.

Ghose, Sri Aurobindo. *The Life Divine.* New York: E. P. Dutton, 1951.

——— *The Synthesis of Yoga.* Pondicherry, India: Sri Aurobindo Ashram, 1971.

——— *The Future Evolution of Man.* Ed. by Saint-Hilaire, P. Pondicherry, India: Sri Aurobindo Ashram, 1963.

Hardin, G. *Exploring New Ethics for Survival.* New York: Viking Press, 1972.

Hillman, J. *ReVisioning Psychology.* New York: Harper & Row, 1975.

Houston, J. *Life Force: The Psycho-Historical Recovery of Self.* New York: Dell Publishing, 1980.

Jonas, H. *The Phenomenon of Life: Toward a Philosophical Biology.* New York: Harper & Row, 1966.

—— *The Gnostic Religion*. Boston: Beacon Press, 1958.

Kant, I. *Grounding for the Metaphysics of Morals*. Trans. by Ellington, J. Indianapolis, Ind.: Hackett, 1981.

Kasulis, T. *Zen Action/Zen Person*. Honolulu: University of Hawaii Press, 1981.

La Chapelle, D. *Earth Wisdom*. Silverton, Col.: Finn Hill Arts, 1978.

Larson, G. "Conceptual Resources in South Asia for 'Environmental Ethics' or The Fly is Still Alive and Well in the Bottle." *Philosophy East and West* 37:150-159.

Lavely, J. "Personalism Supports the Dignity of Nature." *Personalist Forum* 2:21-37.

Livingston, J. *One Cosmic Instant: Man's Fleeting Supremacy*. New York: Houghton Mifflin, 1973.

Macbeth, N. *Darwinism: A Time for Funerals*. Mill Valley, Cal.: Robert Briggs Associates, 1985.

Maitra, S. *The Meeting of the East and West in Sri Aurobindo's Philosophy*. Pondicherry, India: Sri Aurobindo Ashram, 1968.

Manchester, P. "Parmenides and the Need for Eternity." *Monist* Vol. 62, no. 1.

Matter, J. *Love, Altruism, and World Crisis*. Chicago: Nelson-Hall, 1974.

McKinley, D., and Shepard, P., eds. *The Subversive Science*. Boston: Houghton Mifflin, 1969.

Meeker, J. *The Comedy of Survival*. Los Angeles: Guild of Tutors Press, 1980.

Merleau-Ponty, M. *The Primacy of Perception*. Trans. by Edie, J. Evanston, Ill.: Northwestern University Press, 1964.

Nash, R. "Rounding Out the American Revolution: Ethical Extension and the New Environmentalism." *Deep Ecology*. Tobias, M., ed. San Diego: Avant Books, 1985.

Nasr, S. *The Encounter of Man and Nature*. London: Allen & Unwin, 1968.

Passmore, J. *Man's Responsibility for Nature*. London: Duckworth, 1974.

—— "Attitudes Toward Nature." *Nature and Conduct*. Peters, R., ed. London: Macmillan, 1975.

Plotinus. *Enneads*. Trans. by Armstrong, A. Boston: Harvard University Press, 1980-87.

Polanyi, M. *Personal Knowledge*. Chicago: University of Chicago Press, 1958.

—— *The Study of Man*. Chicago: University of Chicago Press, 1959.

Prigogine, I., and Stengers, I. *Order Out of Chaos: Man's New Dialogue with Nature*. New York: Bantam, 1984.

Radhakrishnan, S. *An Idealist View of Life*. Bombay: George Allen & Unwin, 1971.

Raju, P. *Structural Depths of Indian Thought*. Albany, N.Y.: State University of New York Press, 1985.

Regan, T. "The Case for Animal Rights." *In Defense of Animals*. Singer, P., ed. London: Blackwell, 1985.

Rifken, J. *Time Wars: The Primary Conflict in Human History*. New York: Henry Holt & Co., 1987.

Roads, M. J. *Talking With Nature*. Tiburon, CA: H. J. Kramer, 1987.

Rodman, J. "The Liberation of Nature?" *Inquiry* vol. 20, no. 1, 1977.

Routley, R., and V. "Against the Inevitability of Human Chauvinism." *Ethics and the Problems of the Twenty-first Century*. Goodpaster, K., and Sayre, K., eds. Big Bend, Ind.: University of Notre Dame Press, 1979.

Rubinstein, R. *The Cunning of History*. New York: Harper, 1978.

Ruether, R. *Liberation Theology*. New York: Paulist Press, 1972.

Sale, K. *Dwellers in the Land: The Bioregional Vision*. San Francisco: Sierra Club Books, 1985.

Santmire, H. *The Travail of Nature: The Ambiguous Ecological Promise of Christian Theology*. Philadelphia: Fortress Press, 1985.

Scheler, M. *The Nature of Sympathy*. Trans. by Heath, P. Hamden, CT: Archon Books, 1970.

—— *Ressentiment*. Trans. by Holdheim, W. New York: Schocken Books, 1972.

—— *Formalism in Ethics and Non-Formal Ethics of Values*. Trans. by Frings, M., and Funk, R. Evanston, Ill: Northwestern University Press, 1973.

Schneidau, H. *Sacred Discontent: The Bible and Western Tradition*. Berkeley: University of California Press, 1977.

Sessions, G. "*Eco-Philosophy* by Henryk Skolimowski." *Environmental Ethics* 6:167-174.

Shepard, P. *The Tender Carnivore and the Sacred Game.* New York: Charles Scribner's Sons, 1973.

Singer, P. *Animal Liberation.* New York: Avon Books, 1975.

——— *Practical Ethics.* London: Cambridge University Press, 1979.

——— ed., *In Defense of Animals.* London: Blackwell, 1985.

Skolimowski, H. *Eco-Philosophy.* New York: Marion Boyars, 1981.

——— *The Theatre of the Mind.* Wheaton, Ill.: Quest Books, 1984.

——— *Eco-Theology.* Ann Arbor, Mich.: Eco-Philosophy Centre, 1985.

——— "The Dogma of Anti-Anthropocentrism and Eco-philosophy." *Environmental Ethics* 6:280-291.

——— "The Interactive Mind in the Participatory Universe" *World & I.* Washington: Washington Times, February, 1986, pp. 453-470.

Stone, C. *Should Trees Have Standing?: Toward Legal Rights for Natural Objects.* Los Altos, Cal.: W. Kaufmann, 1974.

Swimme, B. *The Universe is a Green Dragon: A Cosmic Creation Story.* Santa Fe, N.M.: Bear & Co., 1985.

Thompson, W. *The Time Falling Bodies Take to Light.* New York: St. Martin's Press, 1981.

Toulmin, S. *The Return to Cosmology: Postmodern Science and the Theology of Nature.* Berkeley: University of California Press, 1982.

Wallis, R. *Neoplatonism.* London: Duckworth, 1972.

Weil, S. *Selected Essays, 1934-43.* Trans. and ed. by Rees, R. London: Oxford University Press, 1962.

Wittgenstein, L. *Tractatus Logico-Philosophicus.* London: Routledge & Kegan Paul, 1961.

Wright, M. *Behaving As If The God In All Life Mattered.* Jeffersonton, VA: Perelandra, 1987.

INDEX